Drawn & colored by Maud Taron

Drawn & colored by Damy Teng

Global Doodle Gems Volume 17
"The Ultimate International Coloring Book...an epic Collection from Artists around the World!"

Drawn & colored by Ellen Wolters

Drawn & colored by Olivia Julius Dunggat

Drawn & colored by Ondine Summers

Drawn & colored by Jenny Wei

Drawn & colored by Andrea Sargent

Drawn by Karim Benyagoub & colored by Elisabeth Delhaye

Drawn by Cynthia Kloeter & colored by Elisabeth Delhaye

Drawn & colored by Wanting Huang

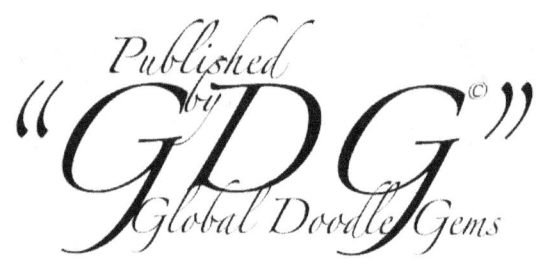

Share your colored versions with us! We love seeing your results and hearing from you we are social!

The Official FB book page, stay on top of what we have in the works !
www.facebook.com/globaldoodlegems
The Community group, share your colored pages, meet the artists, enjoy exclusive freebies, take part in community Charity books and so much more......
www.facebook.com/groups/globaldoodlegems/
Follow us on Twitter.... @GlobalDoodlegem
We are on Instagram too
@globaldoodlegems for instagram
...and if you are not social like that we have a blog
globaldoodlegems.wordpress.com

Copyright © 2016 Global Doodle Gems
All rights are reserved by Global Doodle Gems.
Duplication of pages for personal use are allowed. You are invited to color the pages then scan/post your coloured versions to social networks, mentioning the book title and author/artist (Global Doodle Gems).
All artwork and images are protected by copyright laws. This book or any portion thereof may not, otherwise, be reproduced and/or distributed or transmitted without the express written permission of the artist/publisher of Global Doodle Gems.
All of us from the Global Doodle Gems wish you a colortastic time and look forward to seeing your wonderful color results online !

Contributing Artists

1. Cynthia Kloeter
2. Ellen Wolters
3. Olivia Julius Dunggat
4. Maud Taron
5. Damy Teng
6. Ondine Summers
7. Karim Benyagoub
8. Jenny Wei
9. Andrea Sargent
10. Wanting Huang

Contributing Artist
Cynthia Kloeter
USA

Facebook : CynthiaKloeter

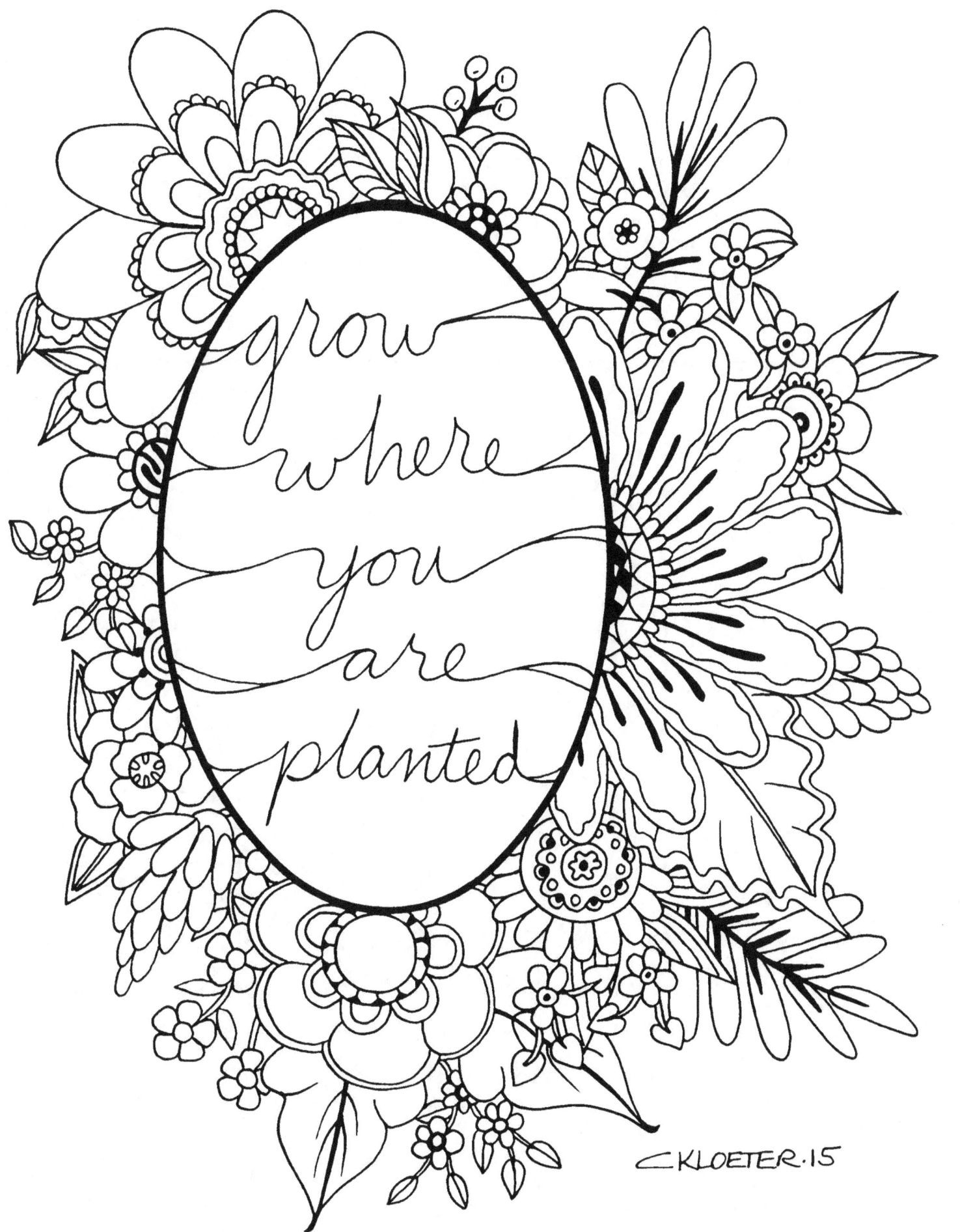

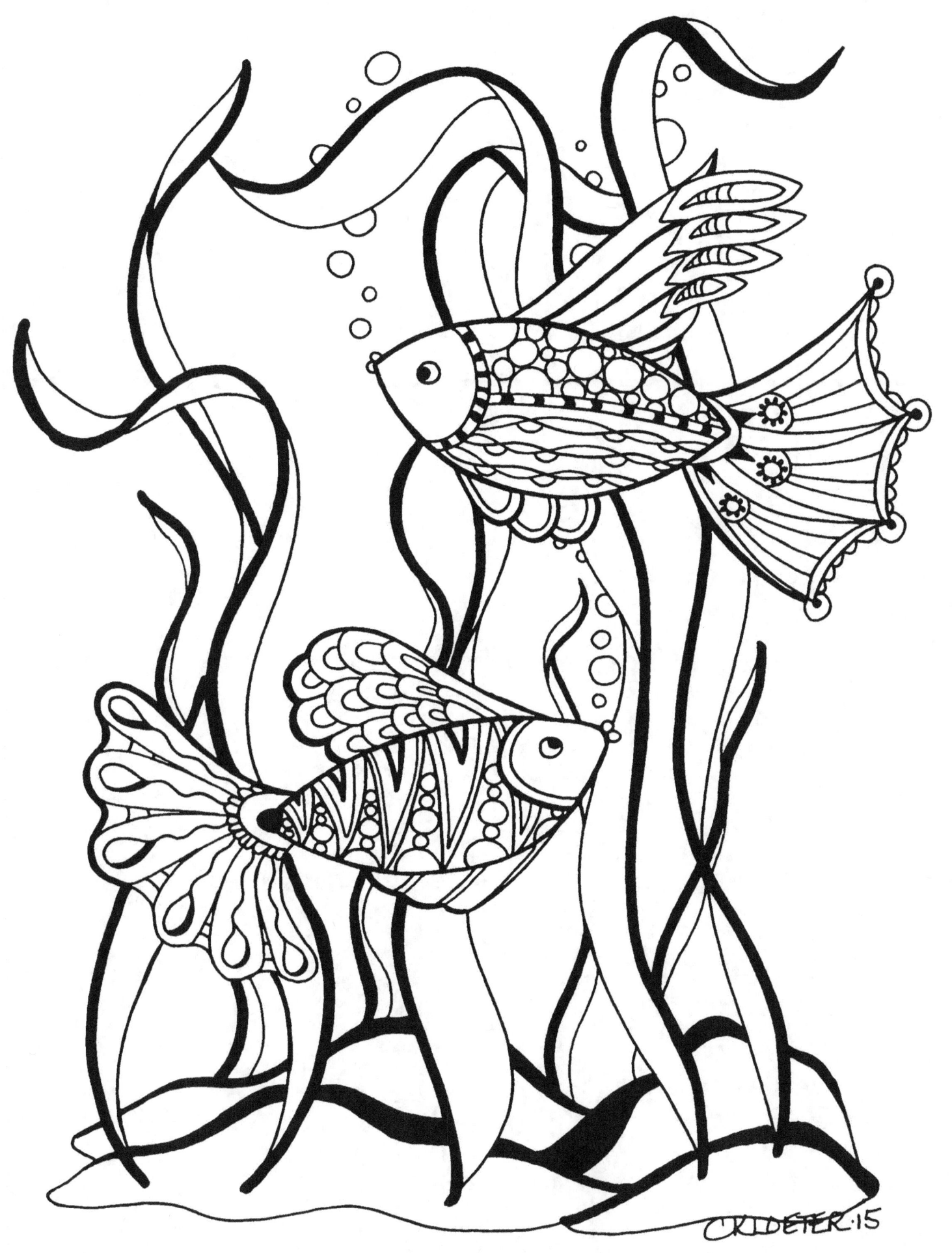

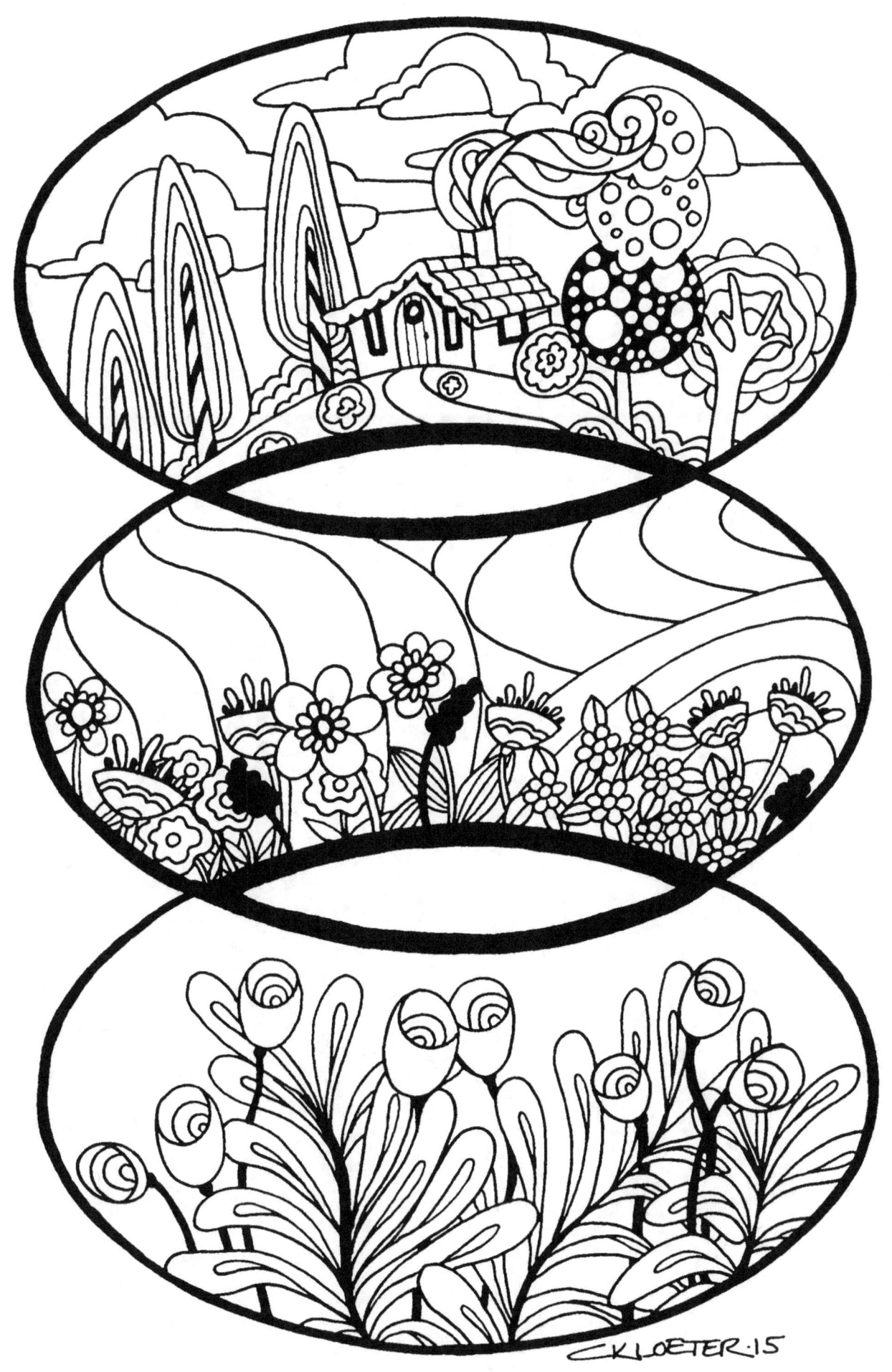

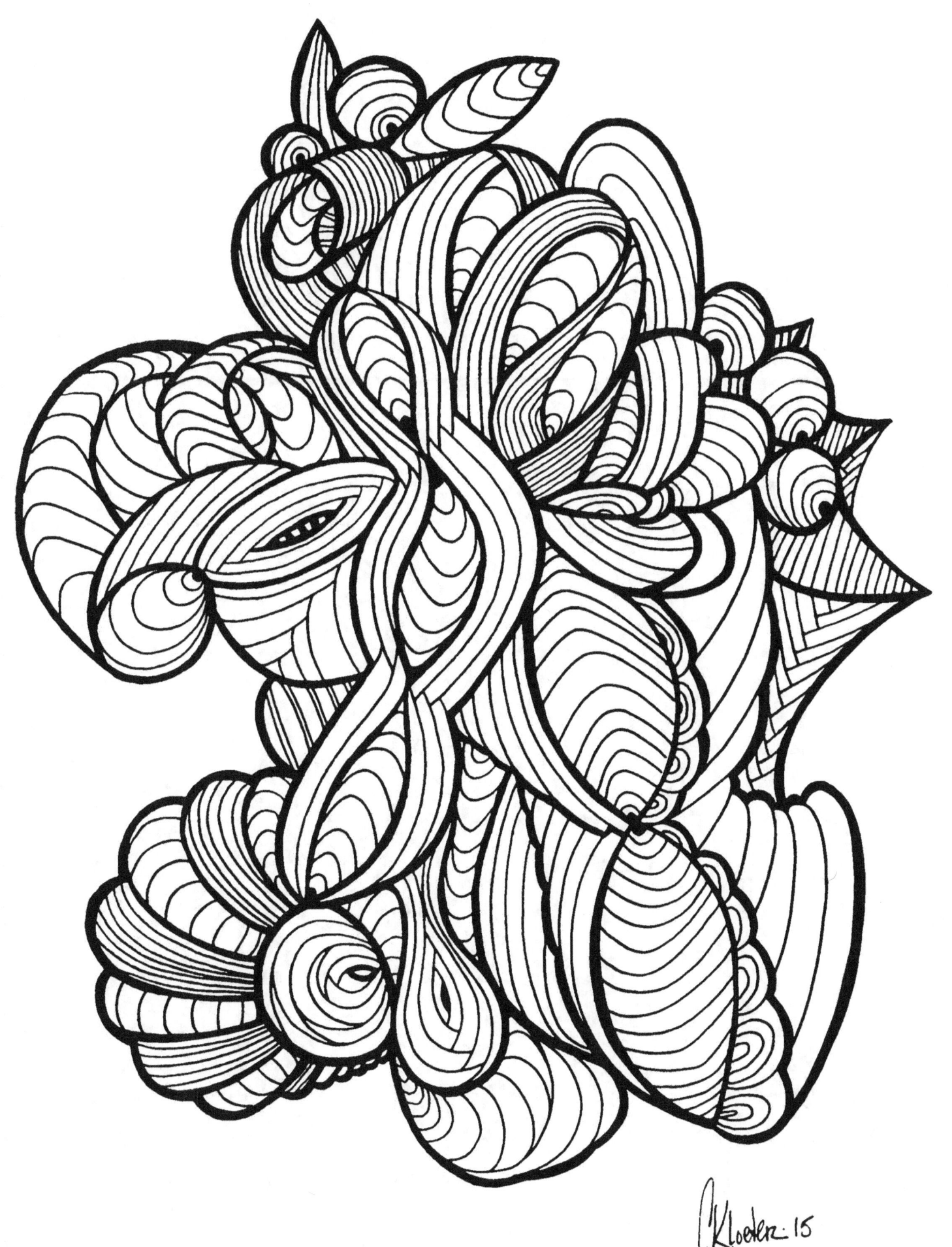

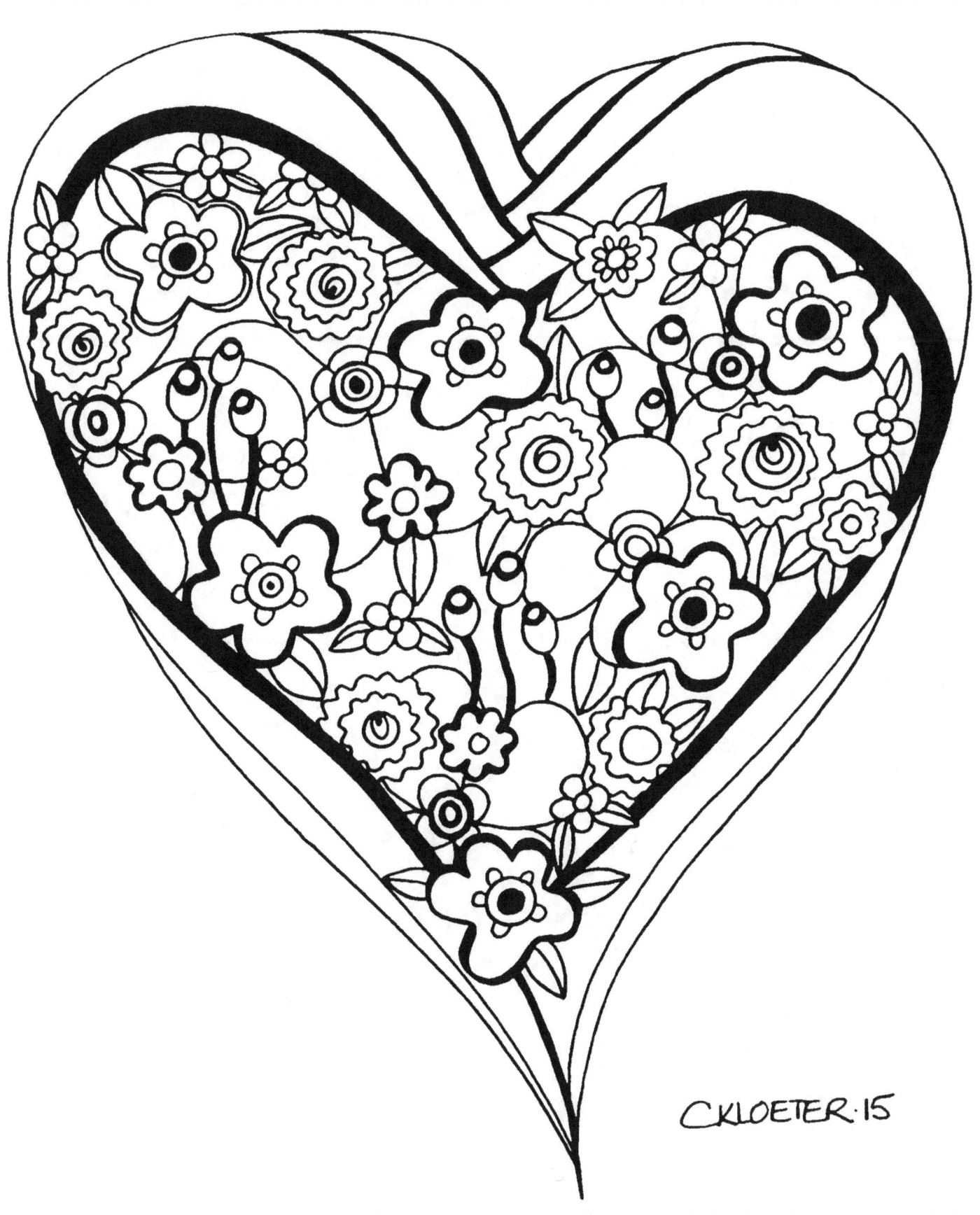

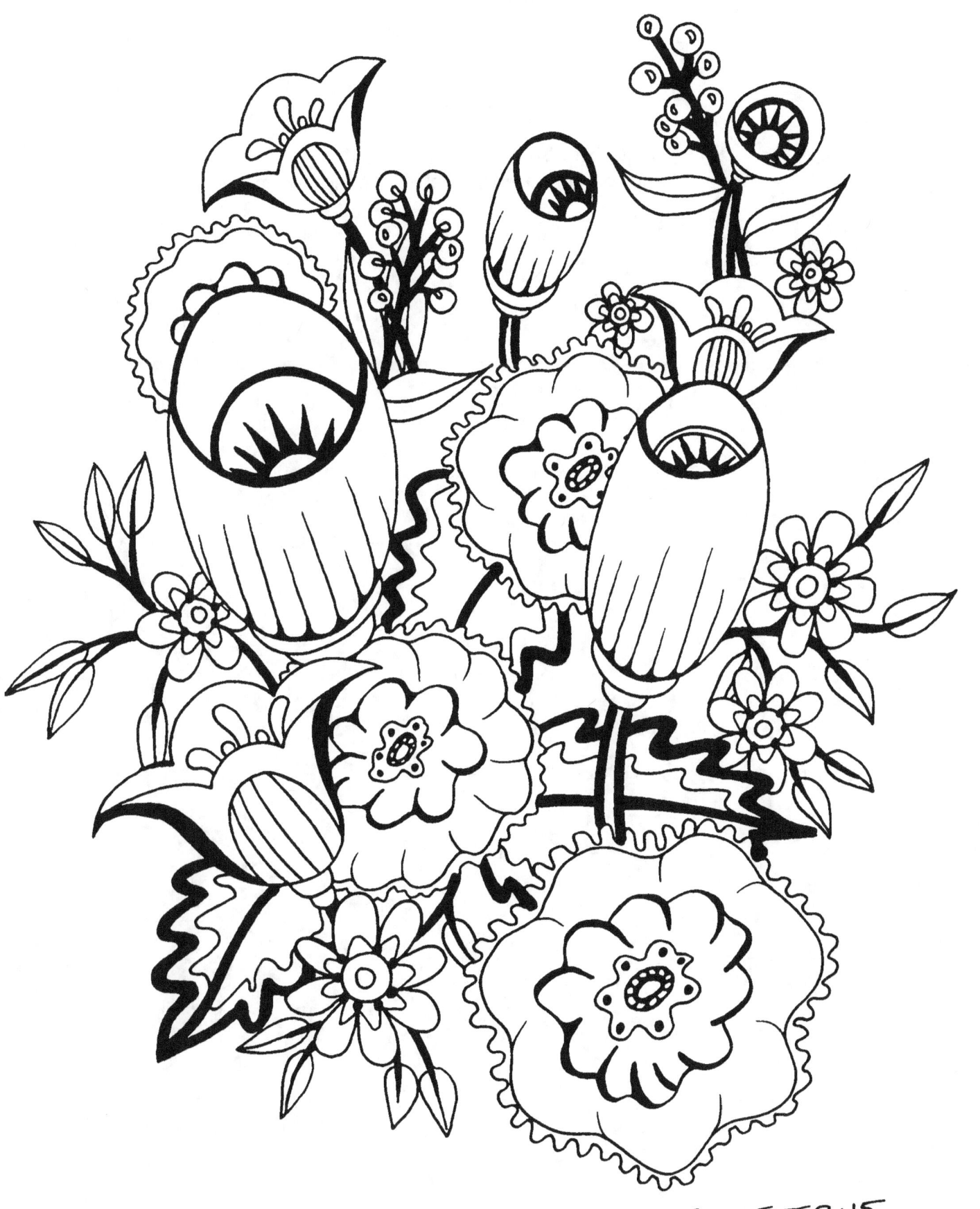

Contributing Artist
Ellen Wolters
The Netherlands

www.ellenstraties@blogspot.com
www.tekenpraktijkdeinnerlijkewereld.blogspot.com

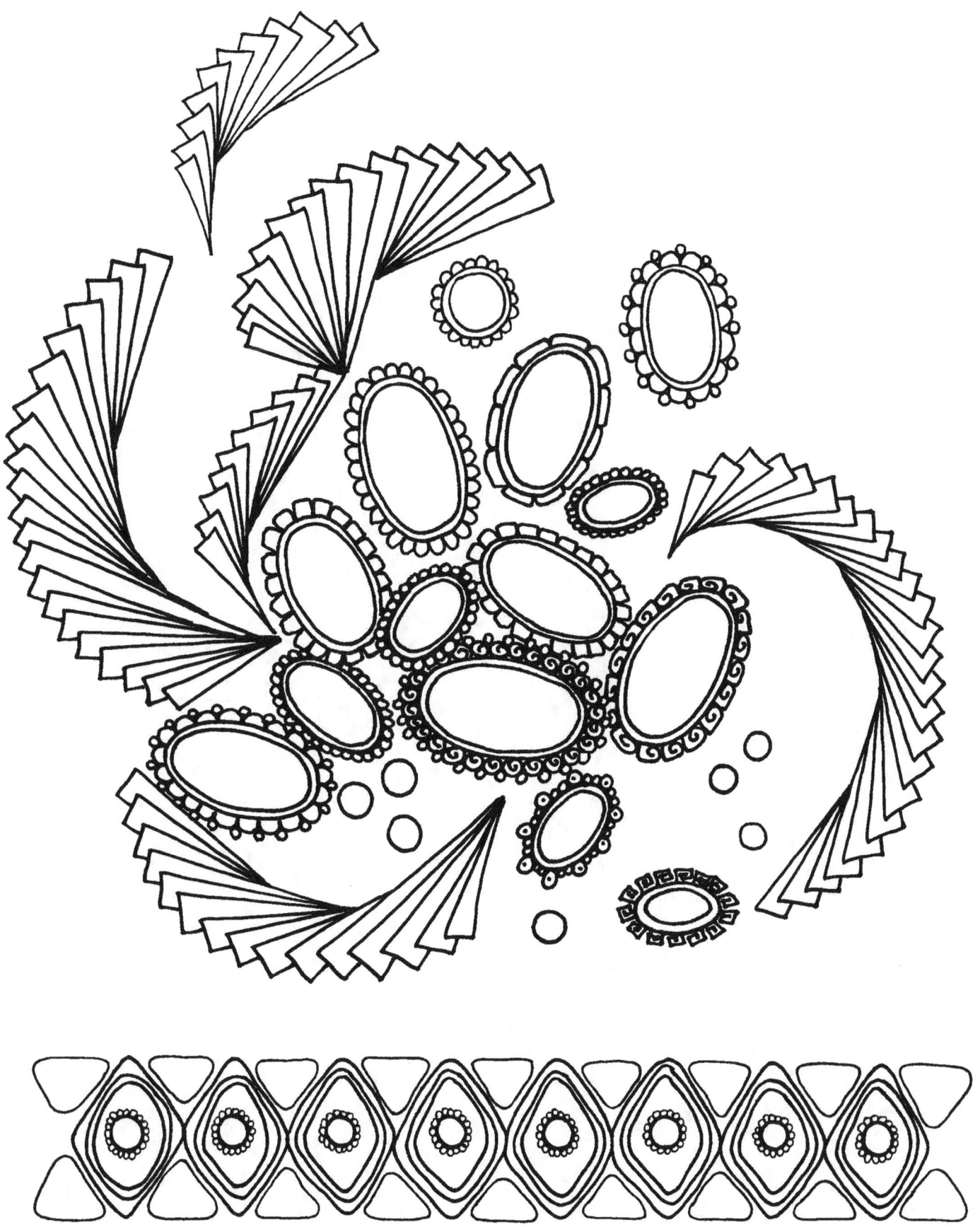

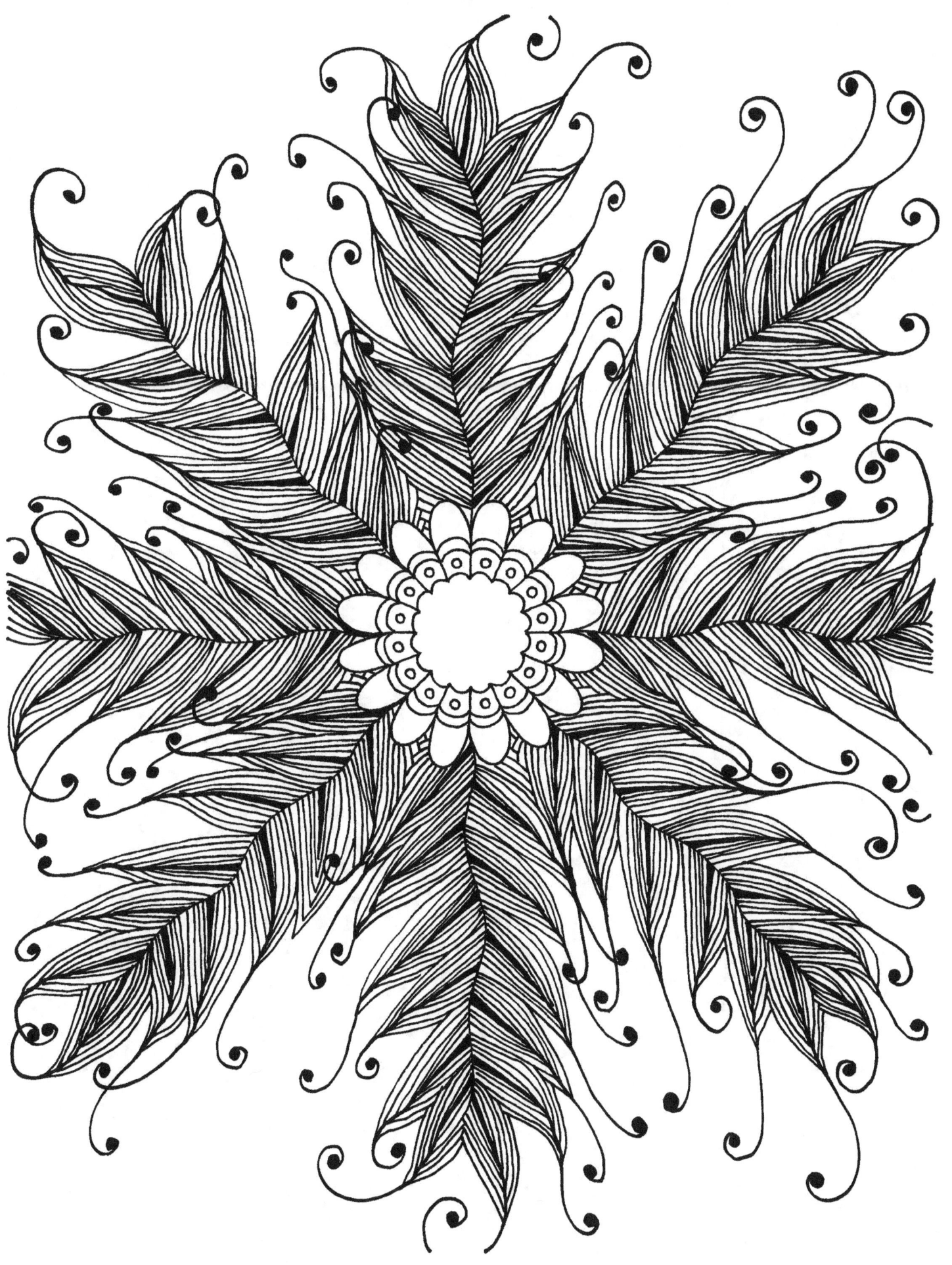

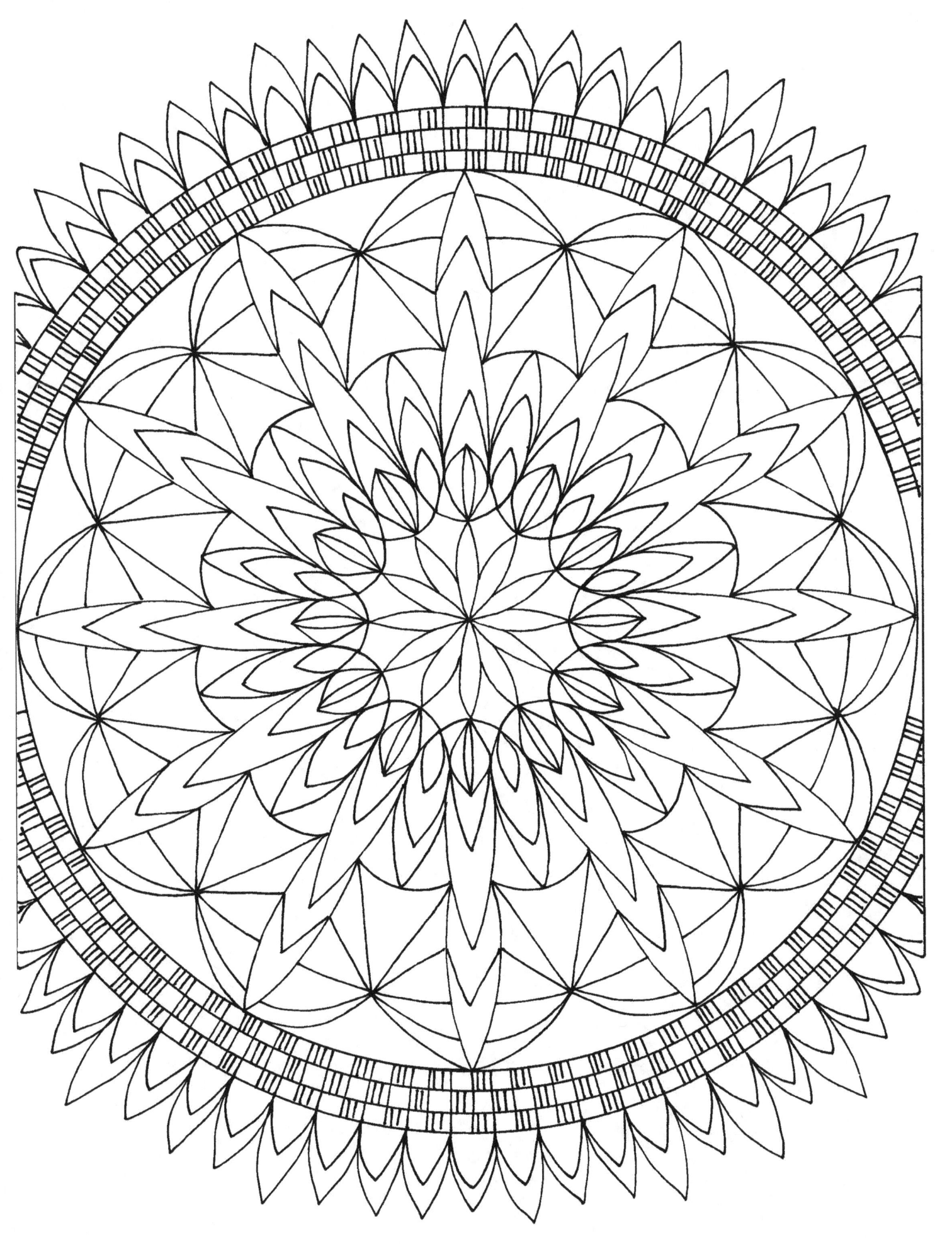

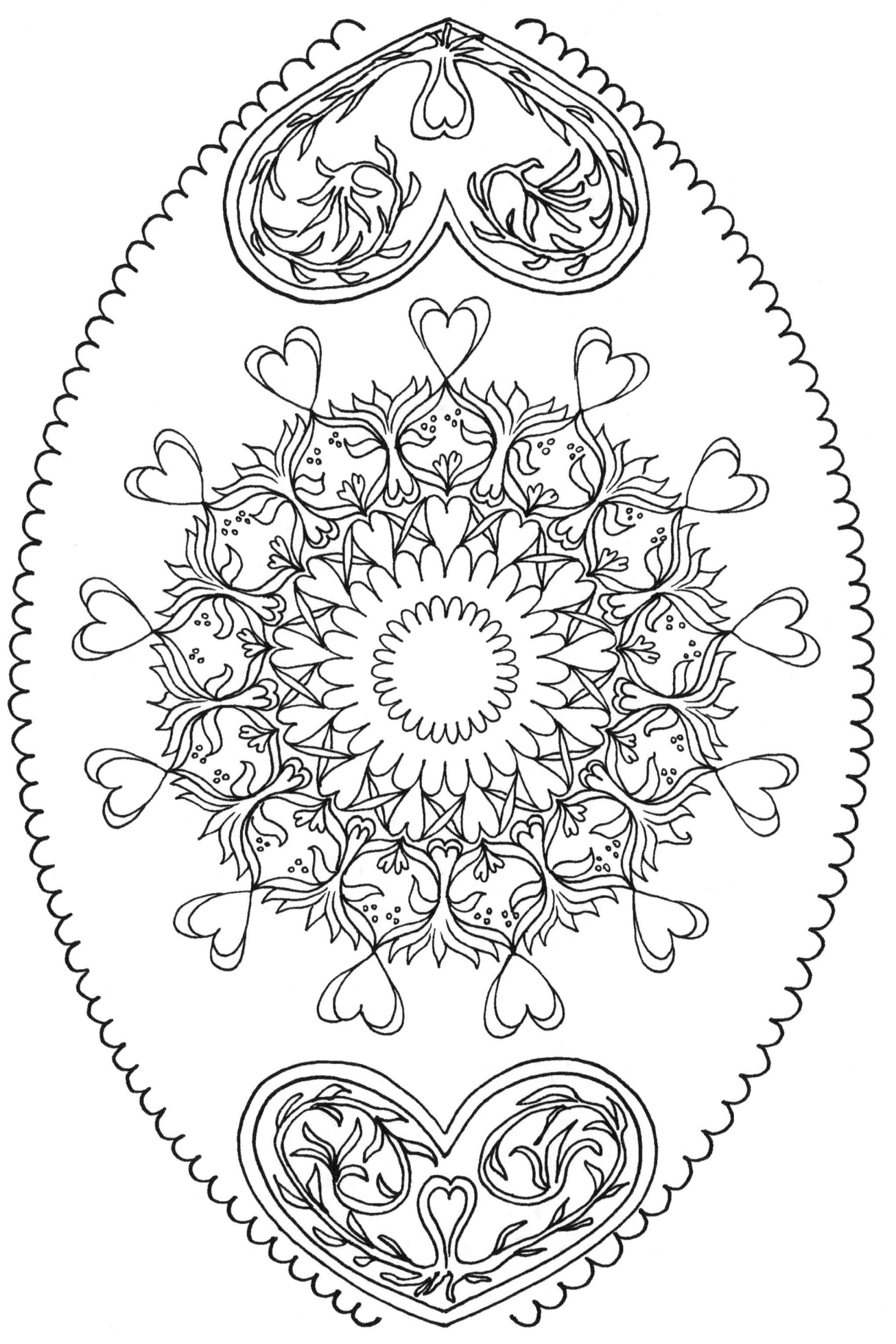

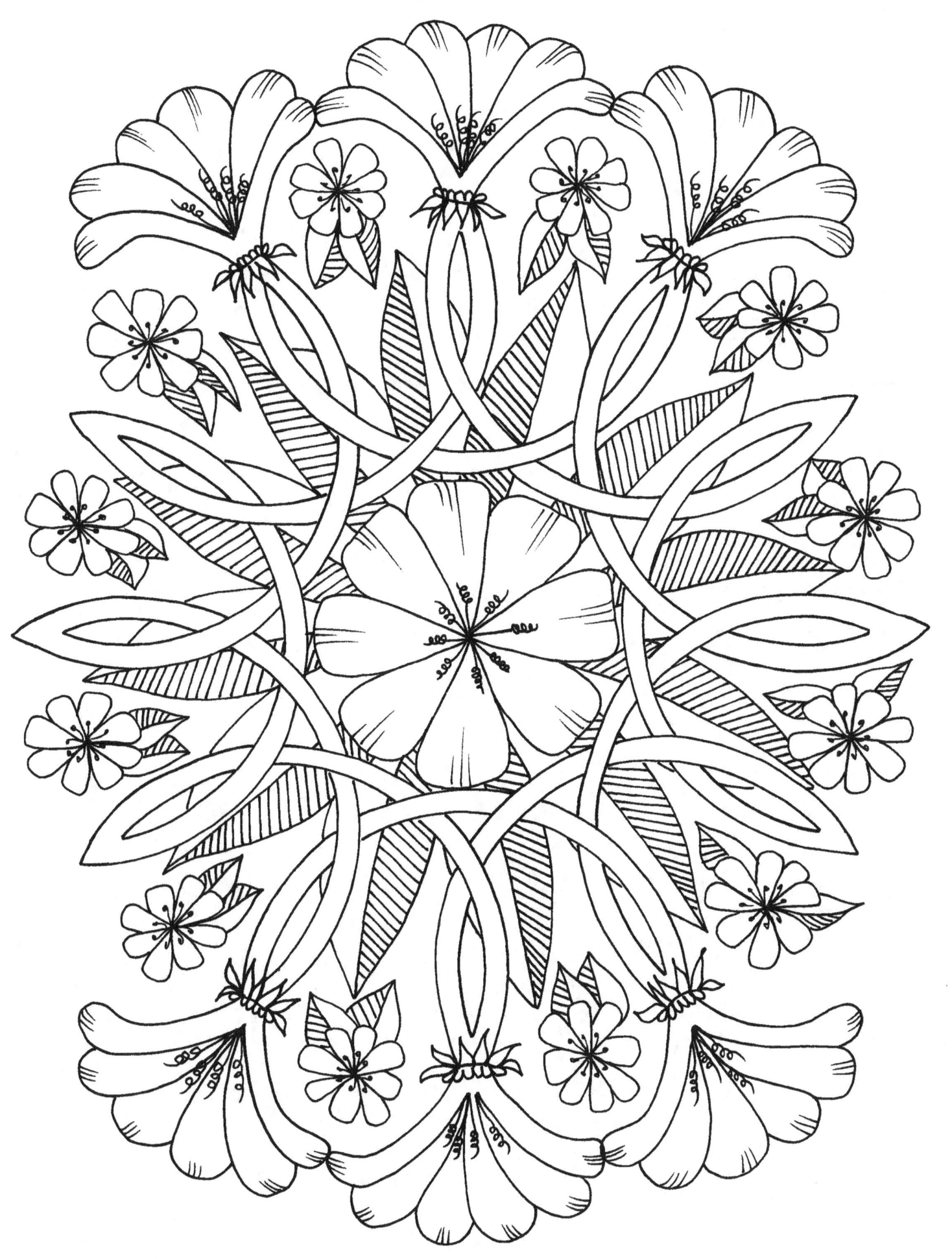

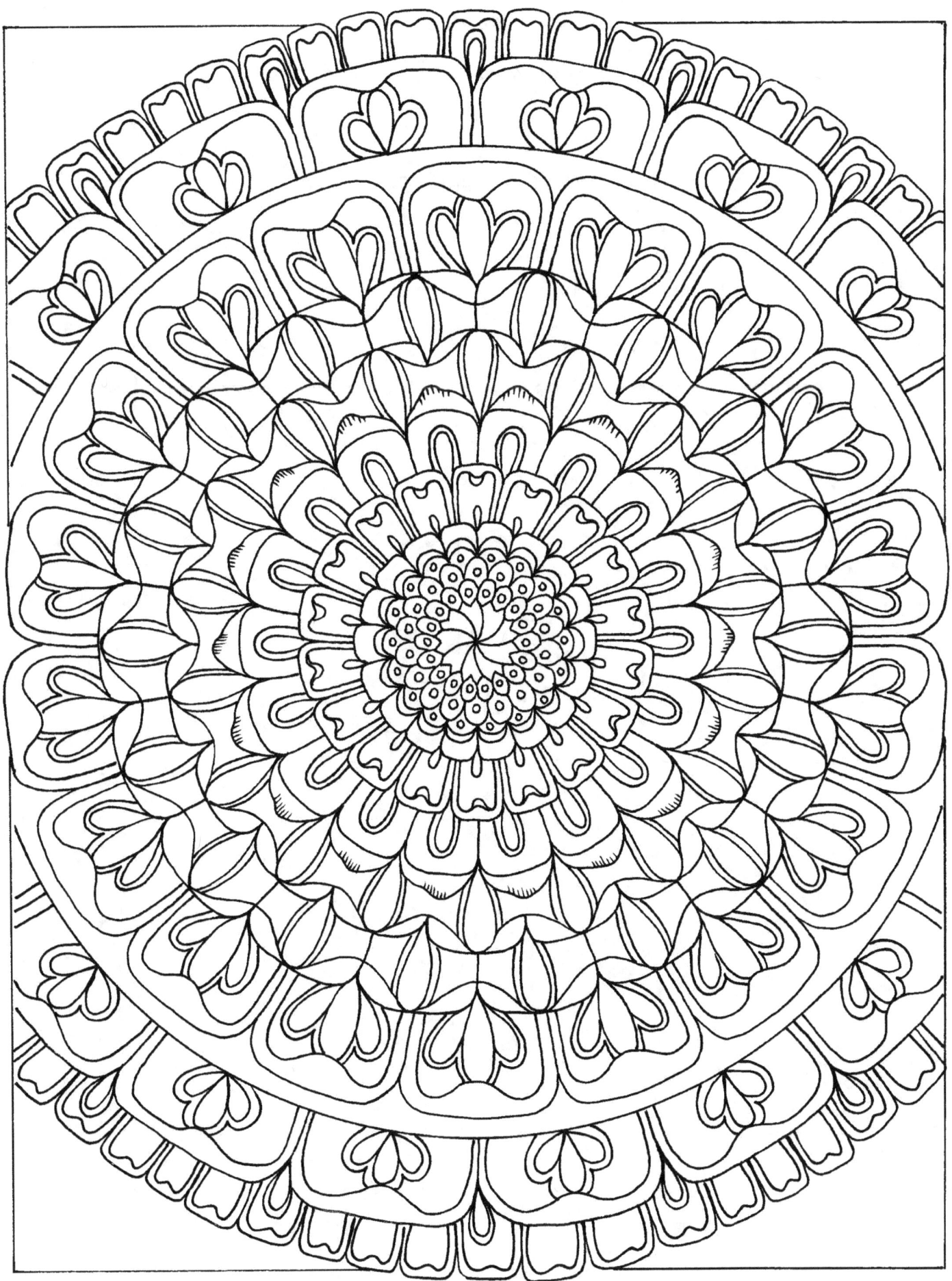

Contributing Artist
Olivia Julius Dunggat
Malaysia

www.coloringiship.com

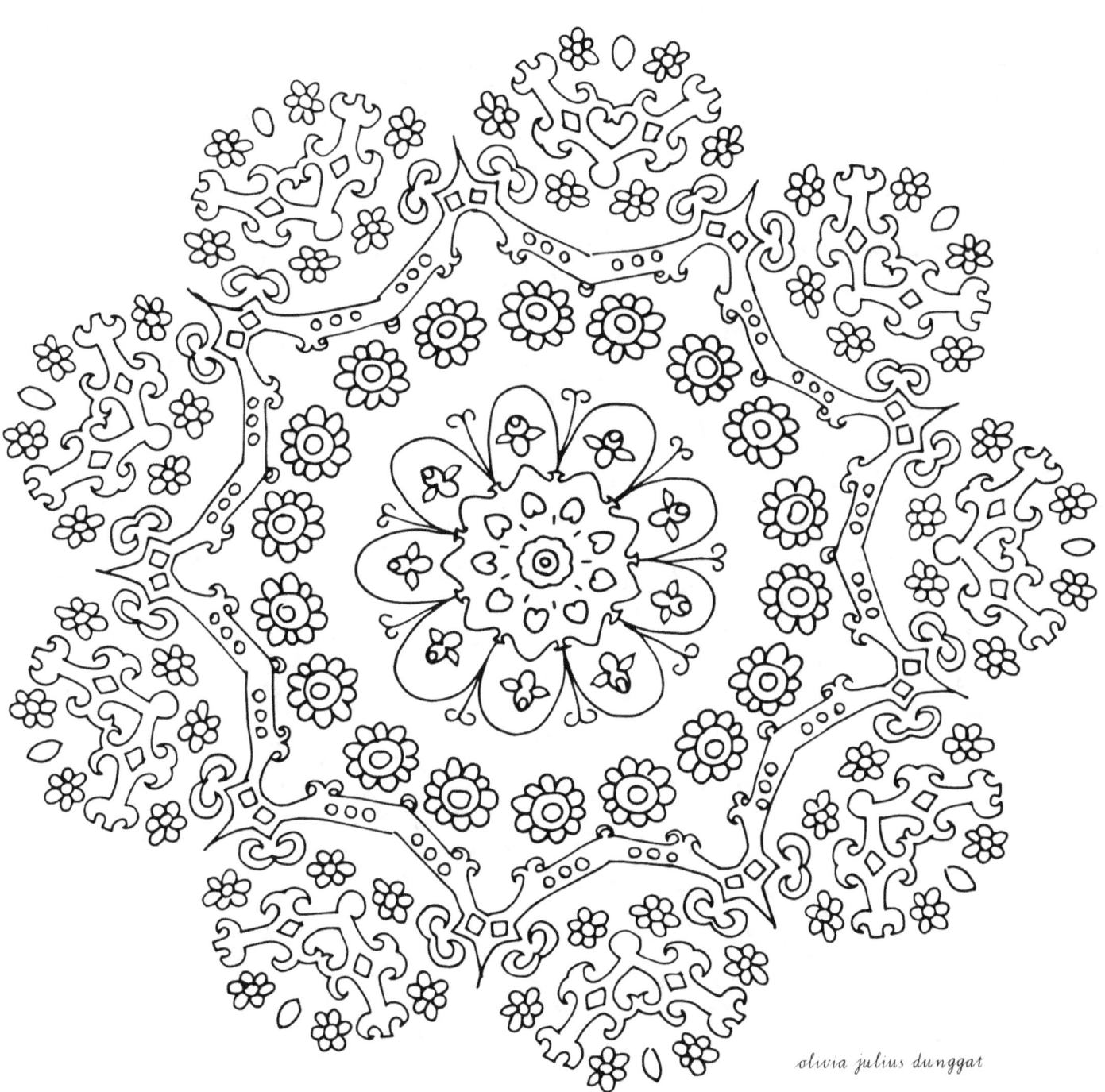

olivia julius dunggat

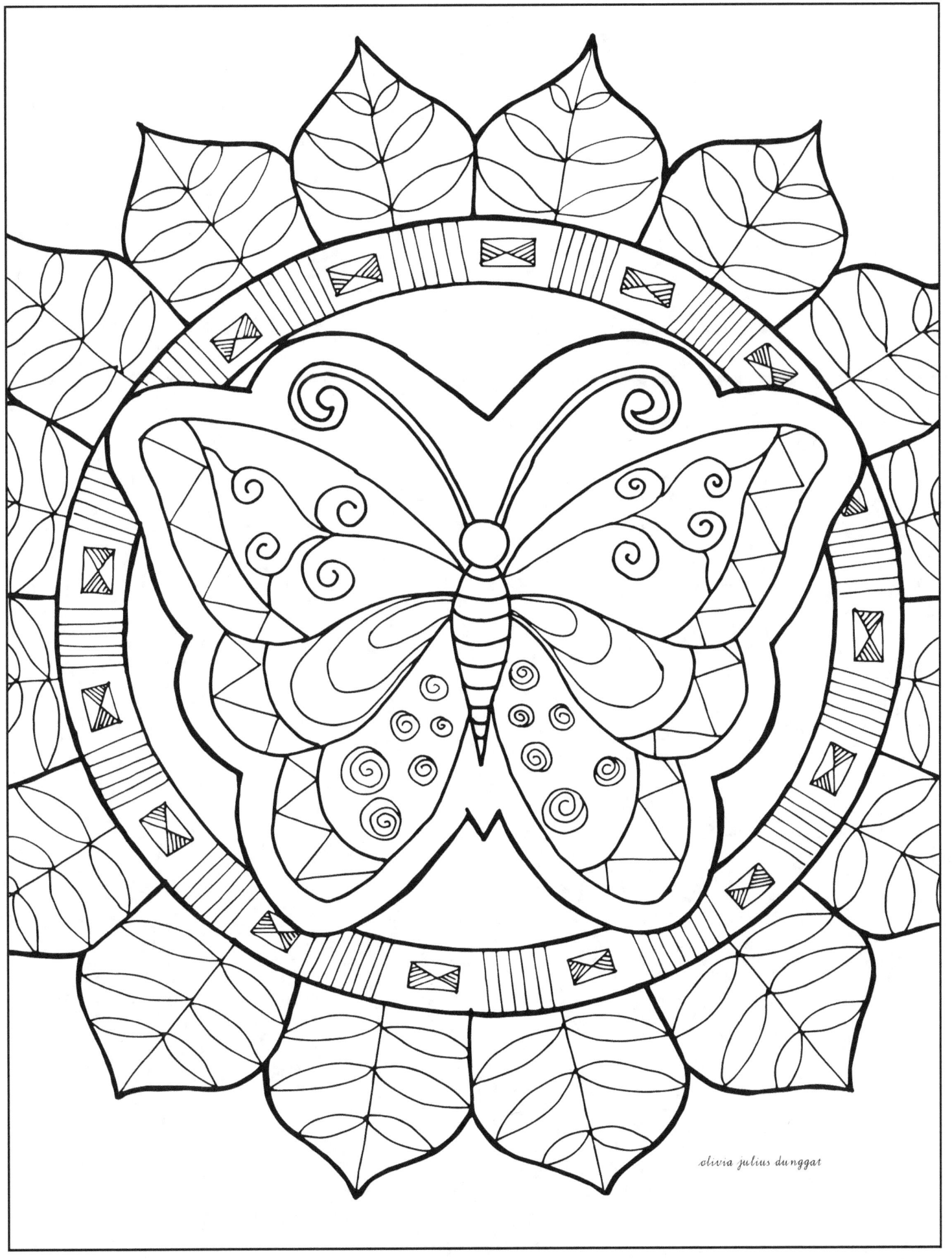

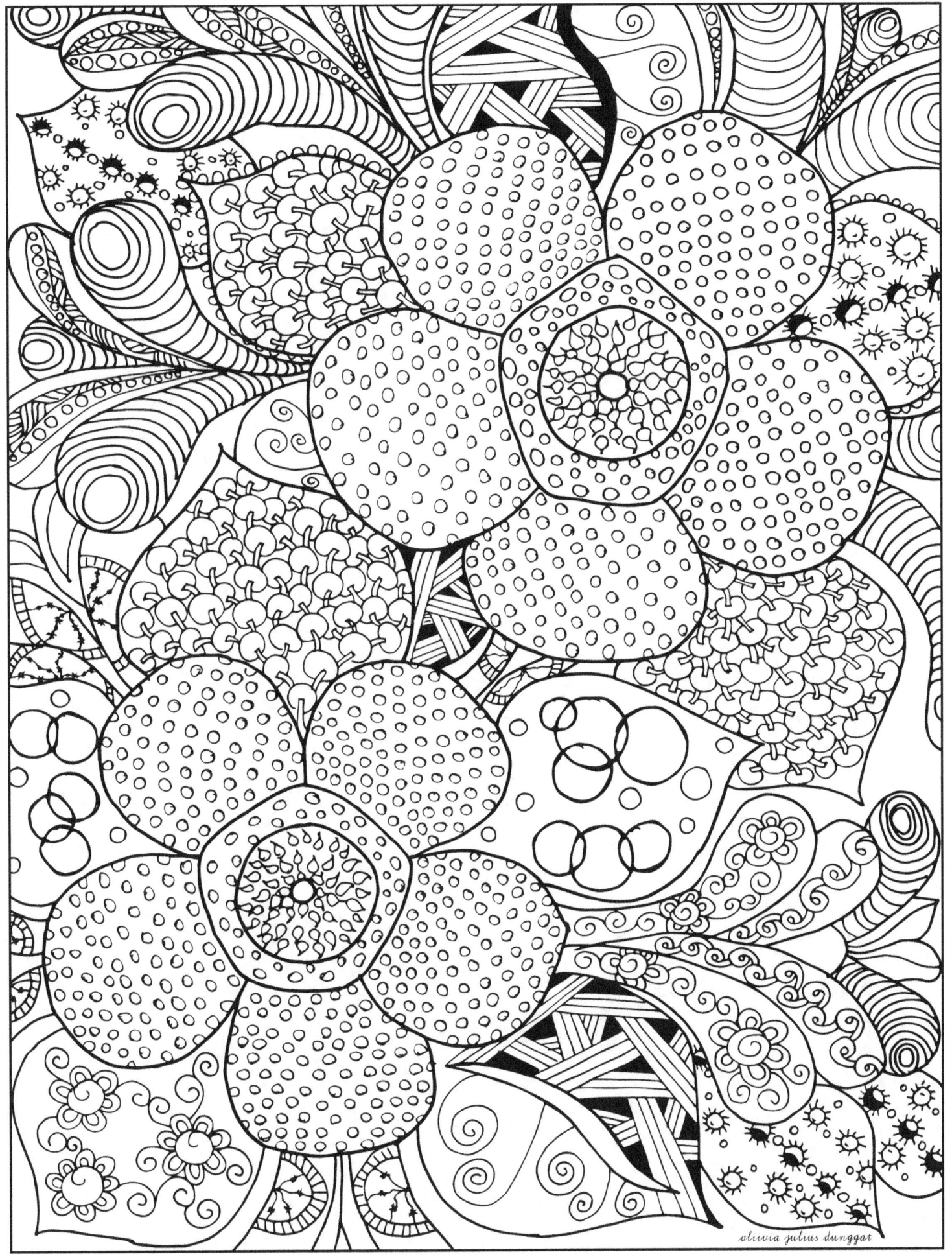

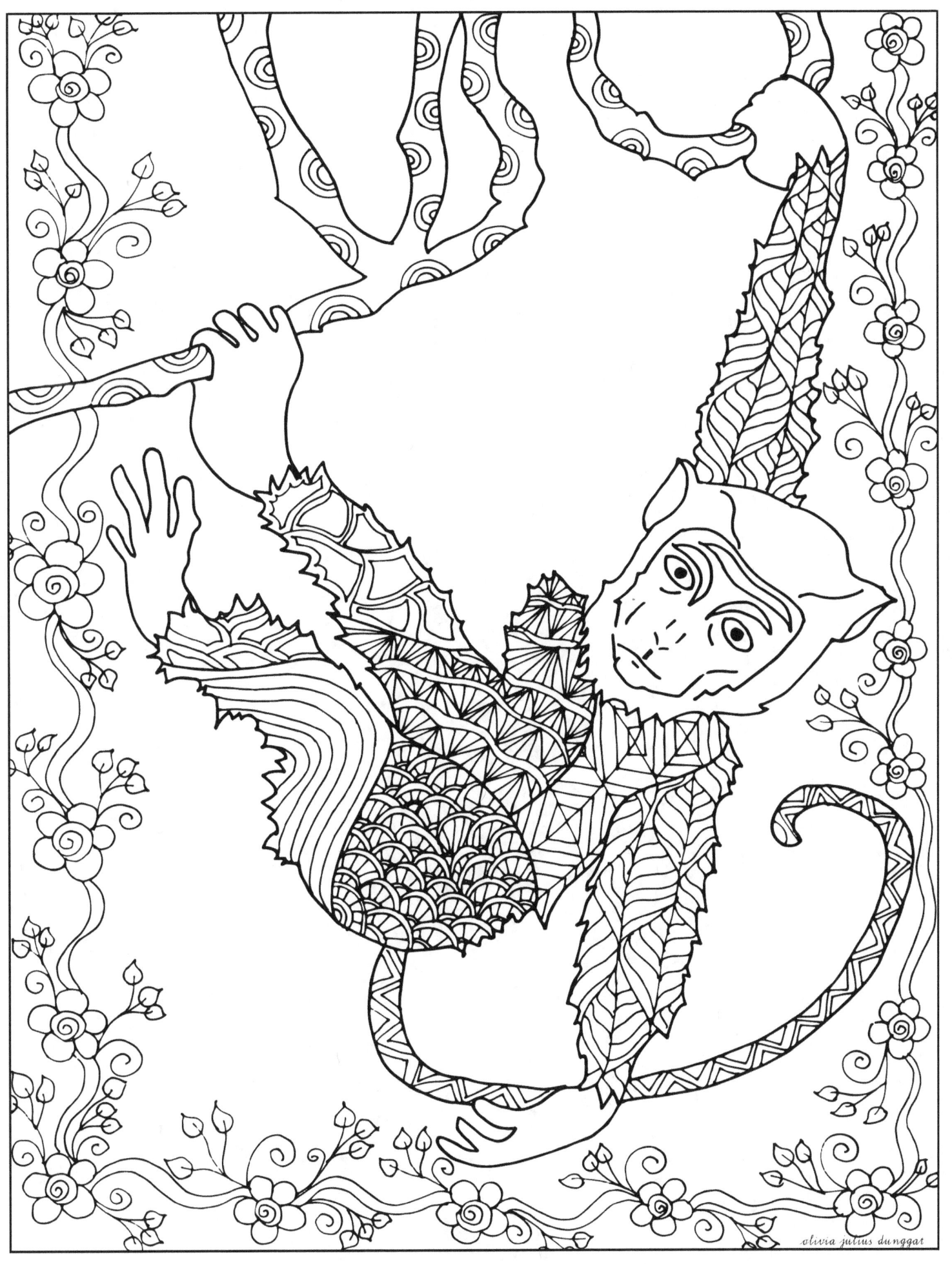

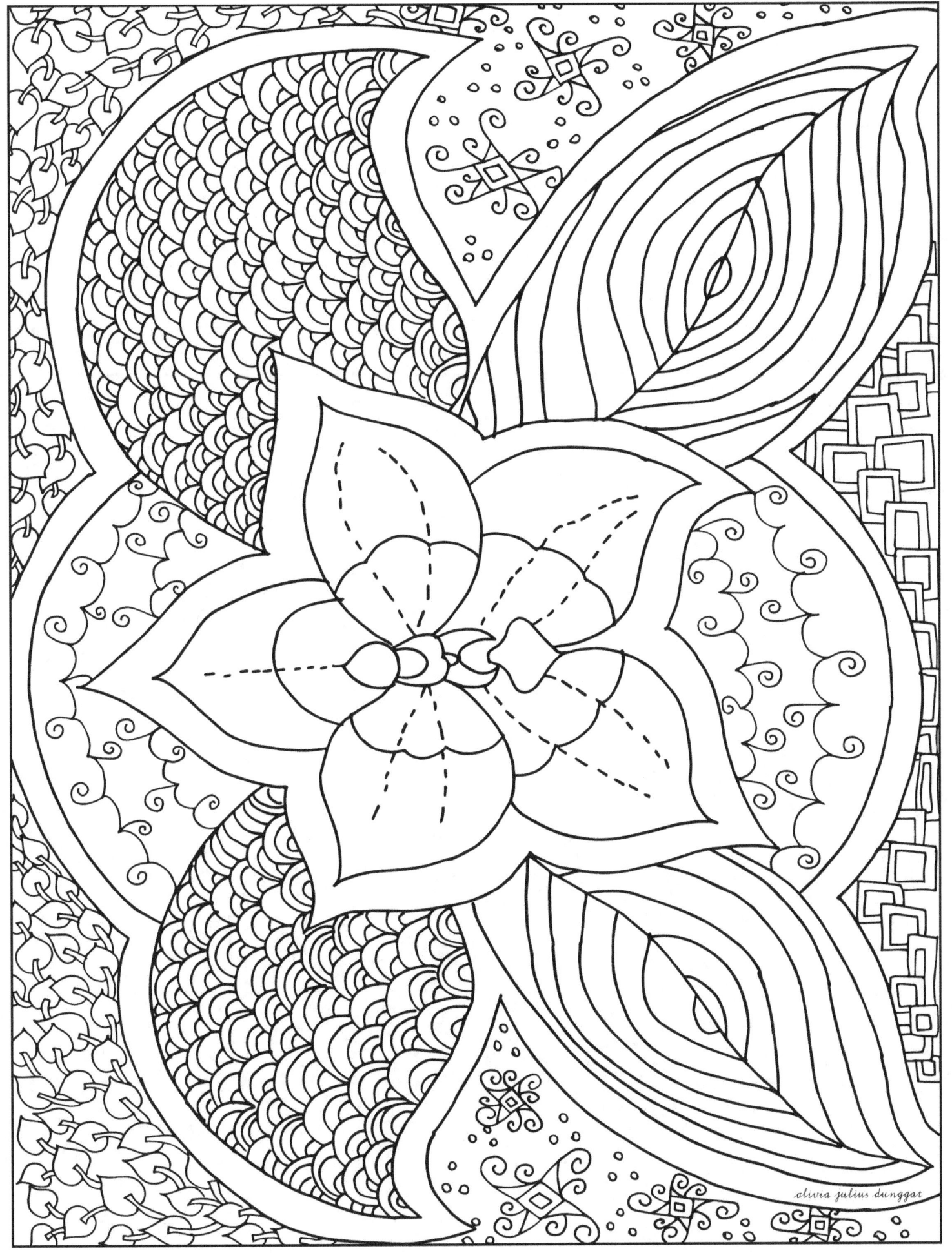

Contributing Artist
Maud Taron

France

Web : www.zendessin.com
Facebook : zendessin
YouTube : http://www.youtube:com/c/MaudT
Instagram : zendessin.maud
Pinterest : http://www.pinterest.com/taleque/
Shop : http://www.etsy.com/fr/shop/TalequeShop
More Books : http://www.amazon.fr/Maud-Taron/e/B00QN8FGJS

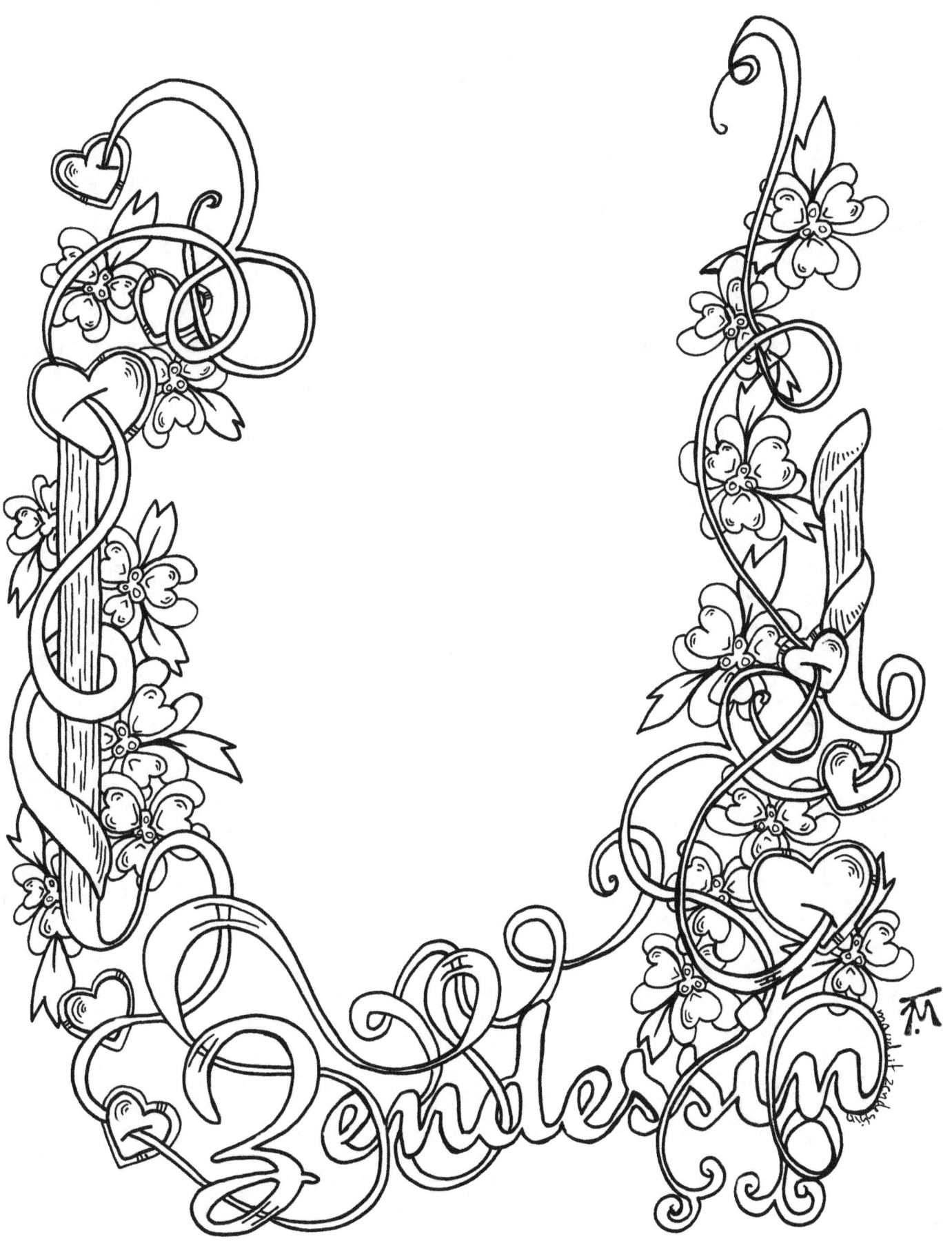

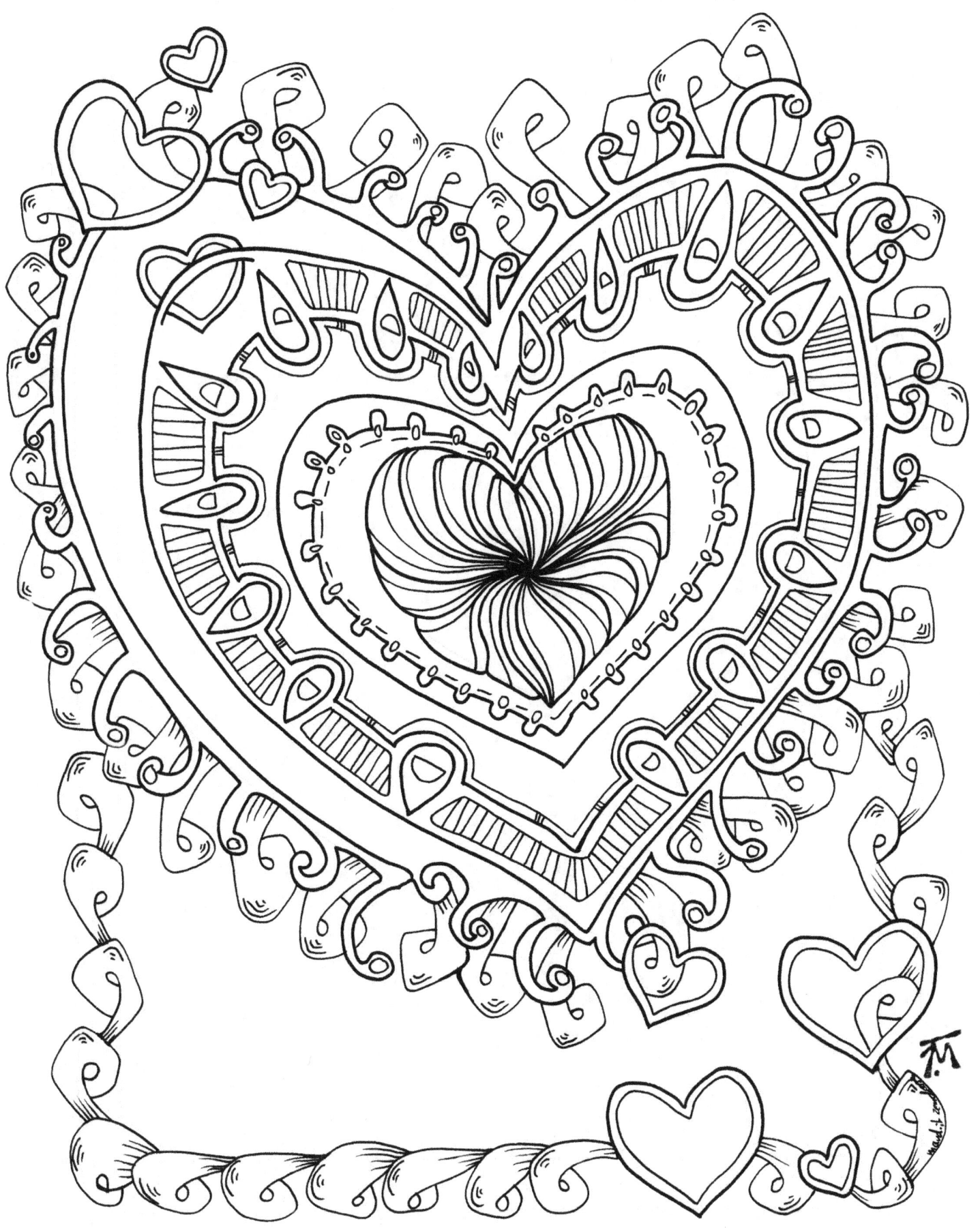

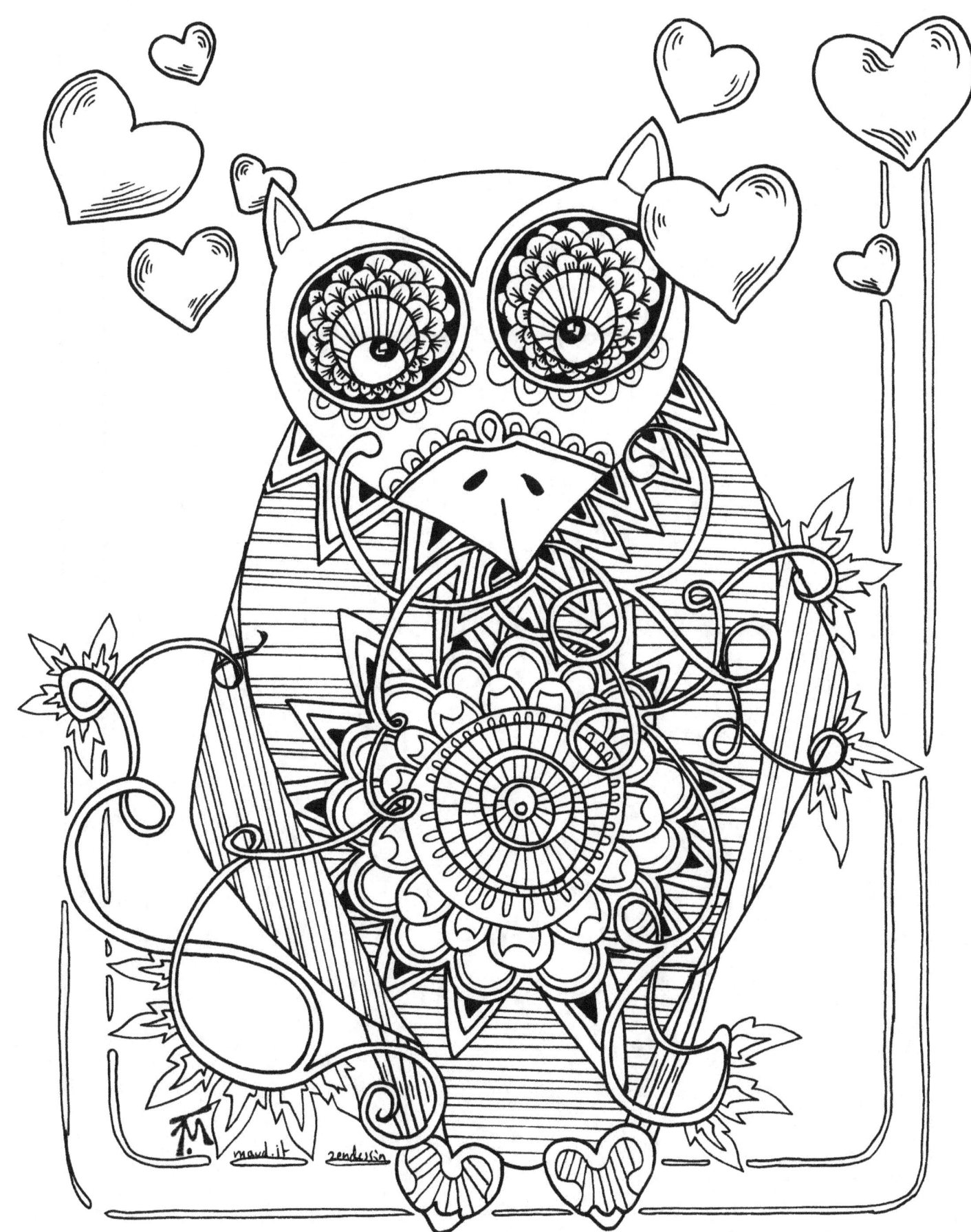

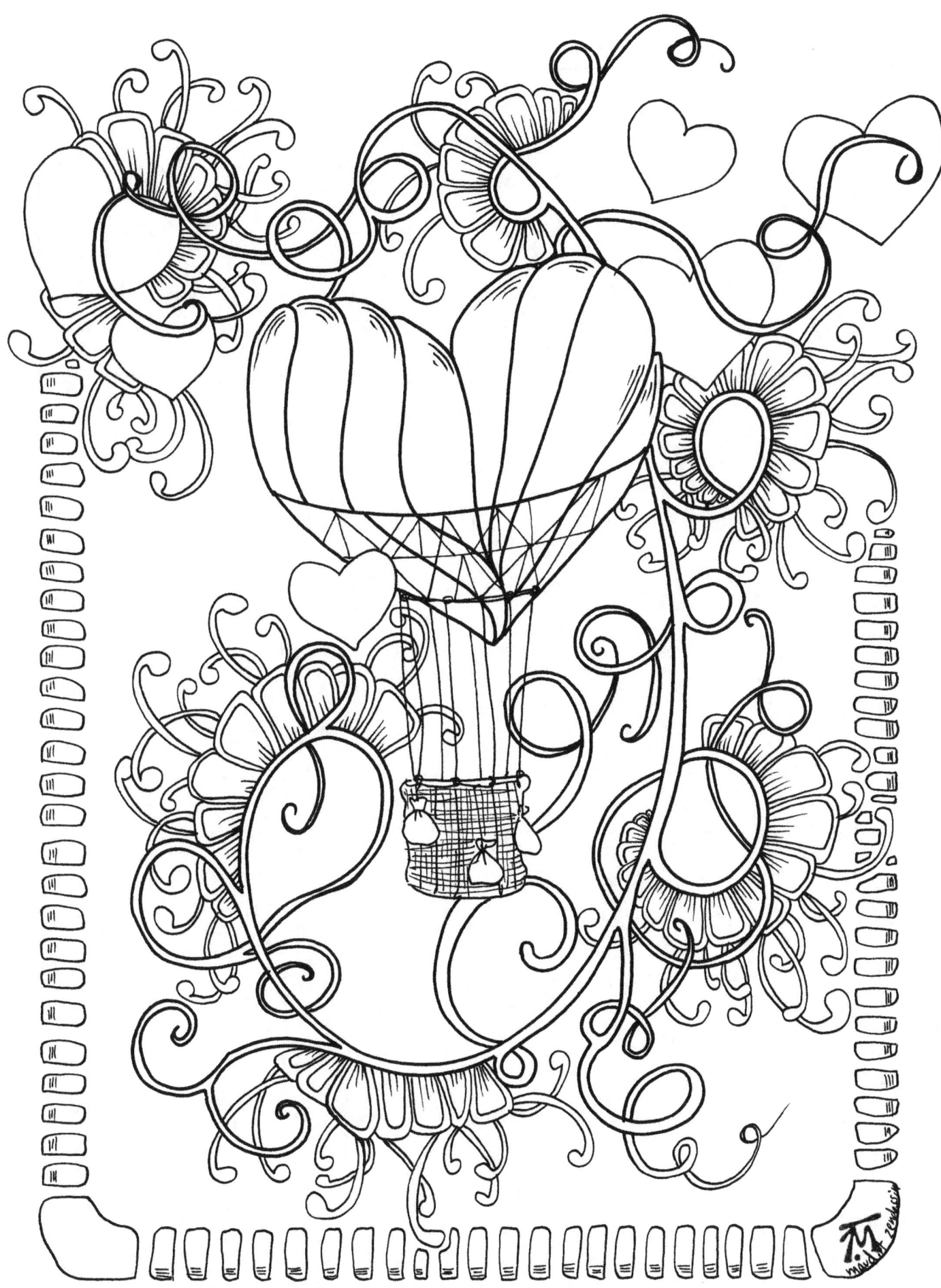

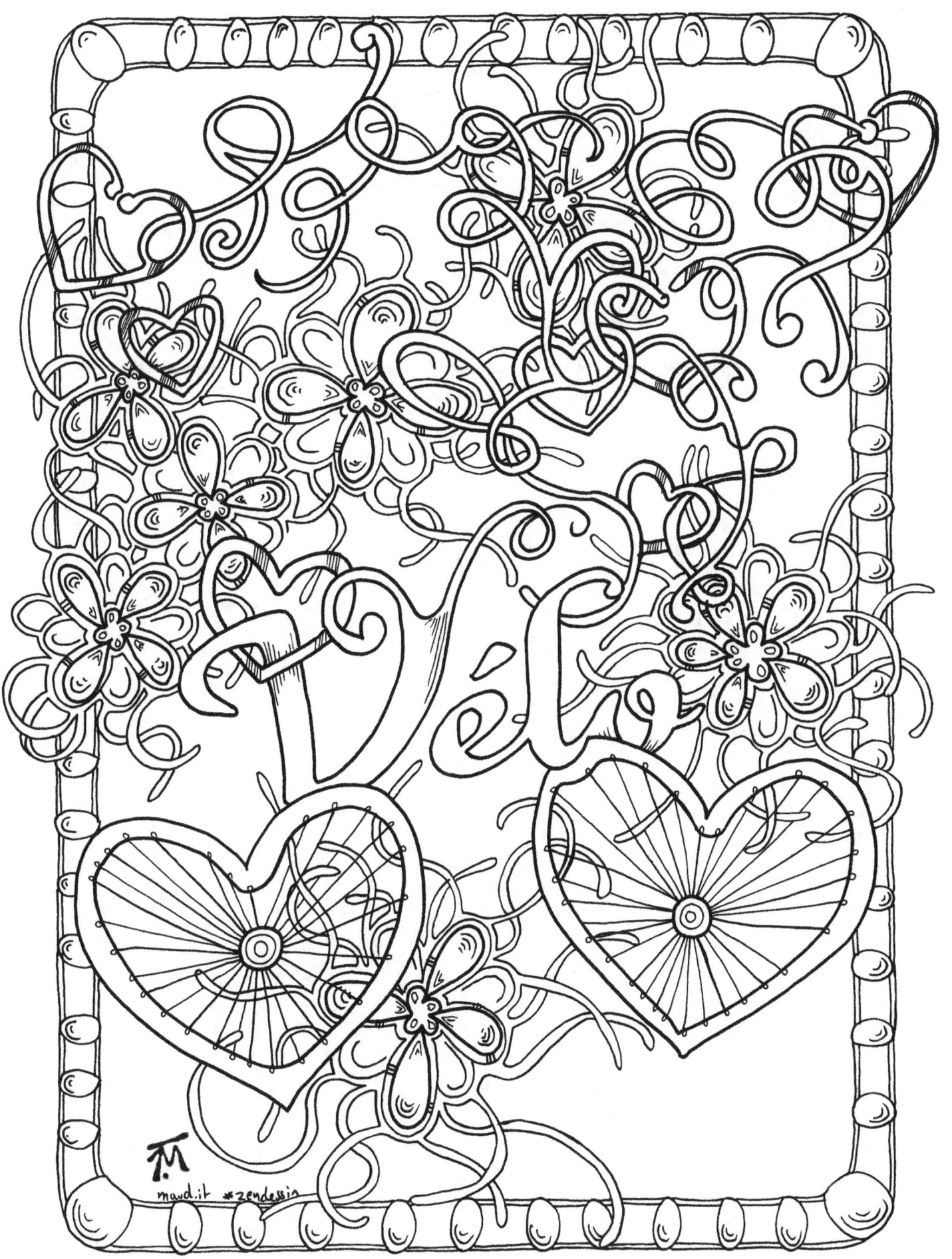

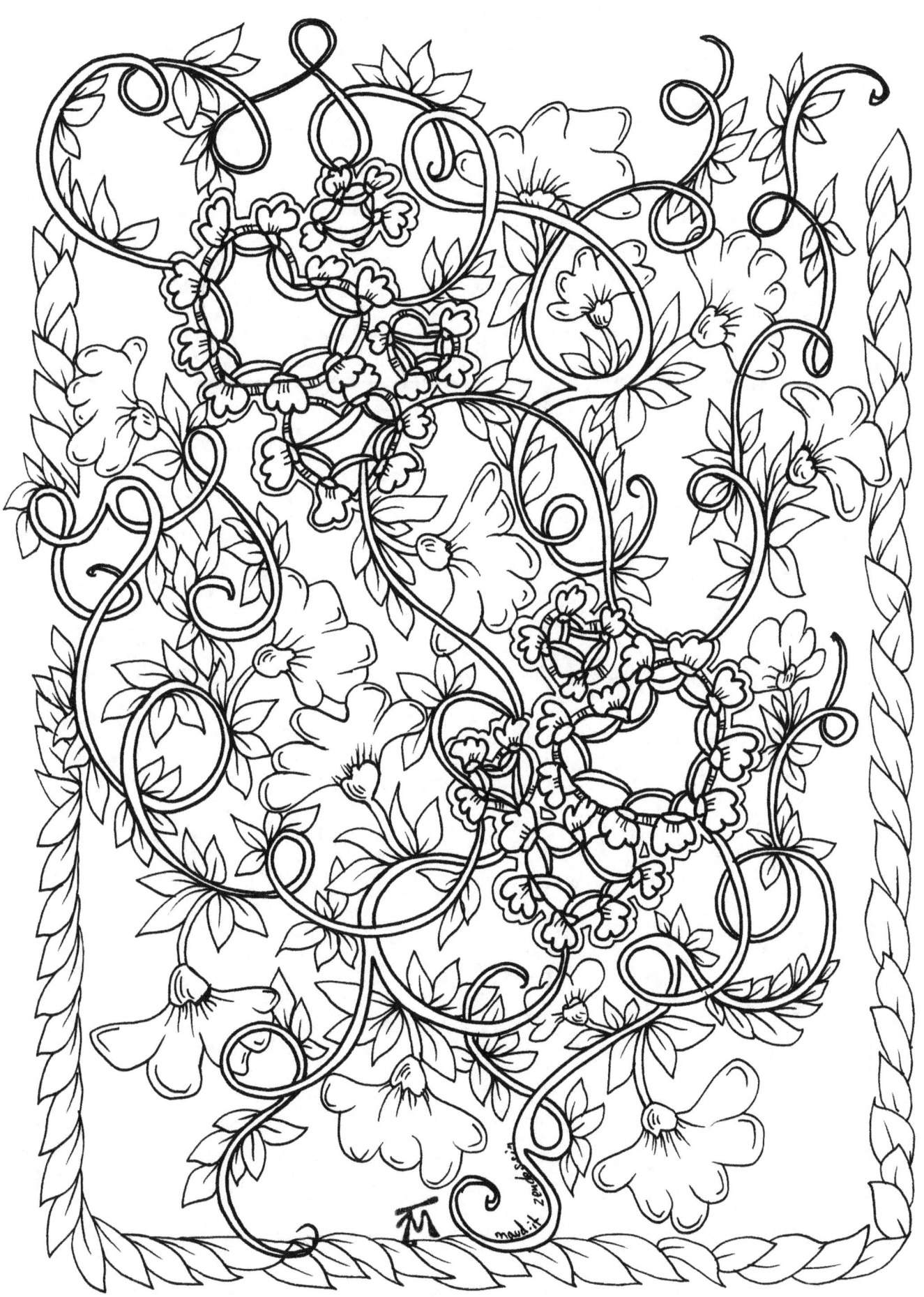

Contributing Artist
Damy Teng
Taiwan

Facebook : damy779

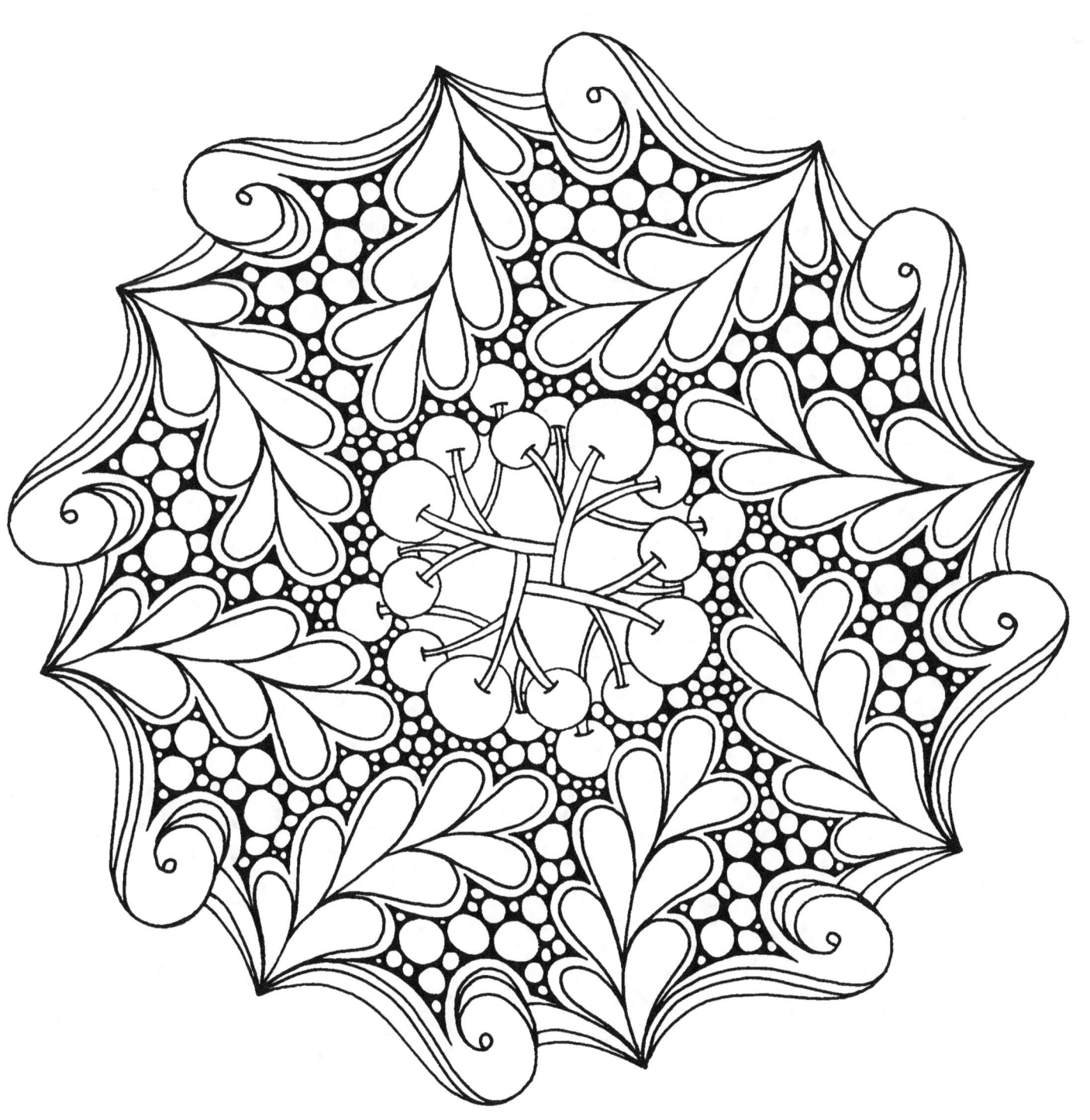

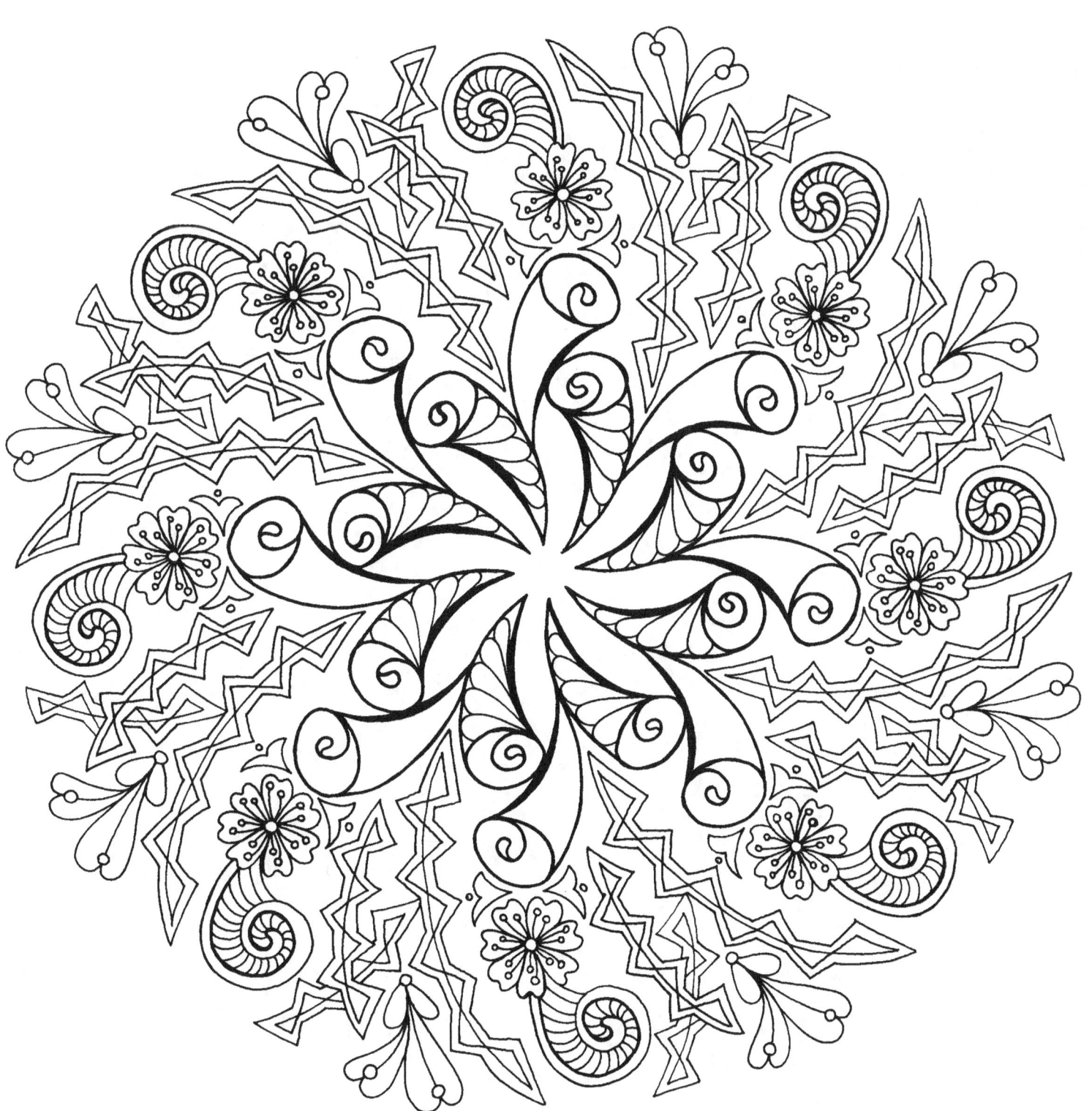

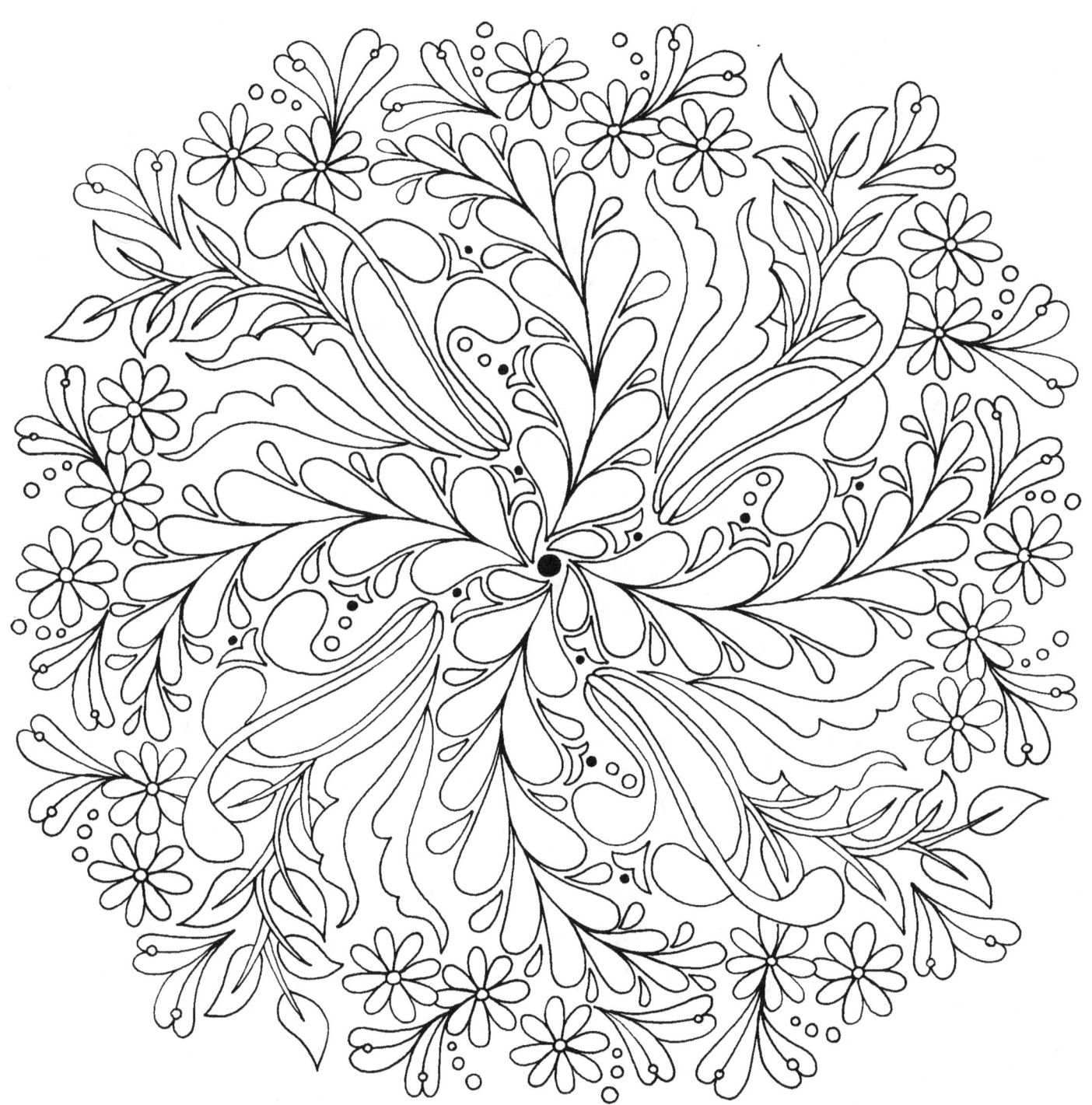

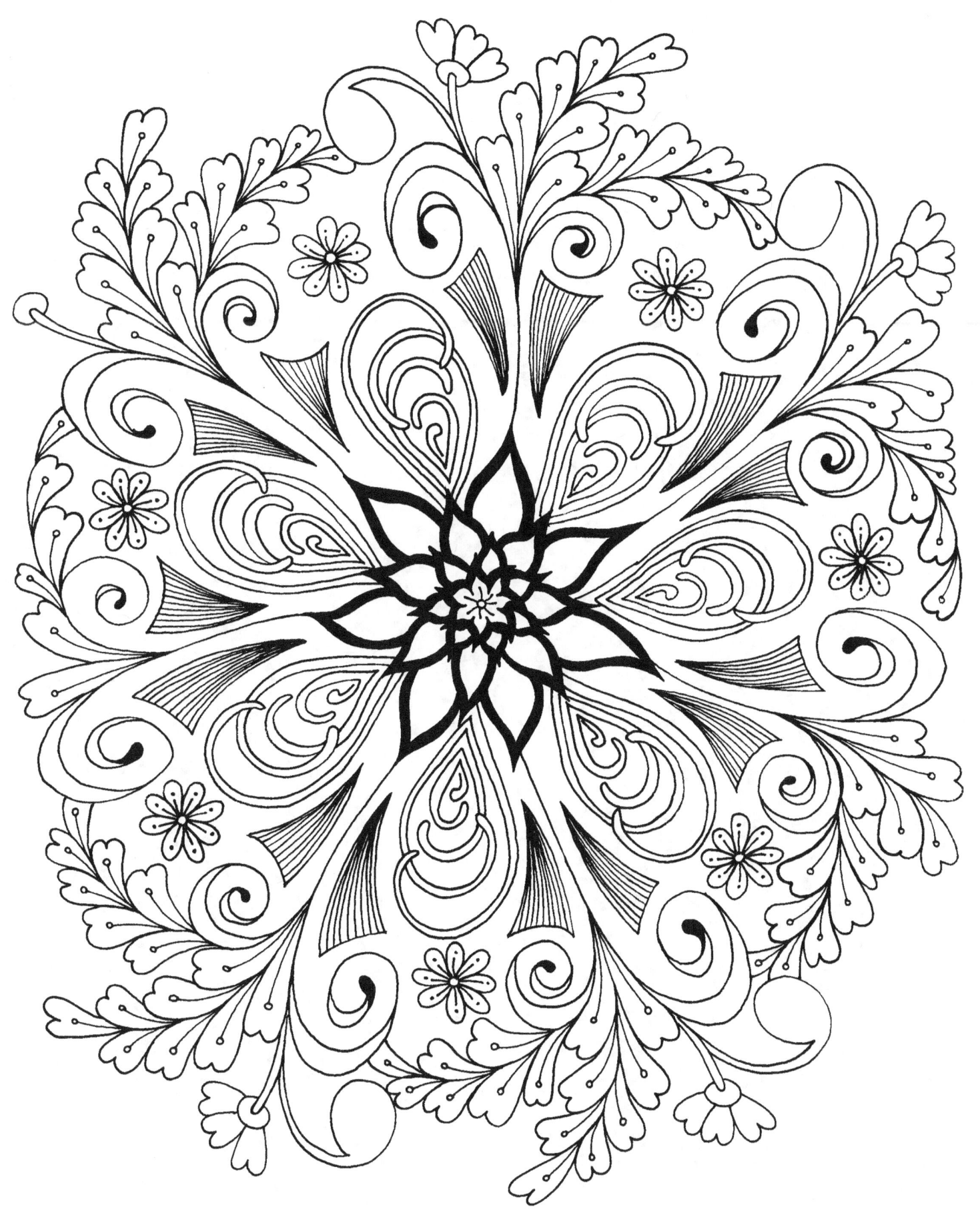

Contributing Artist
Ondine Summers
England

Facebook : colourit
Etsy : Colour it books

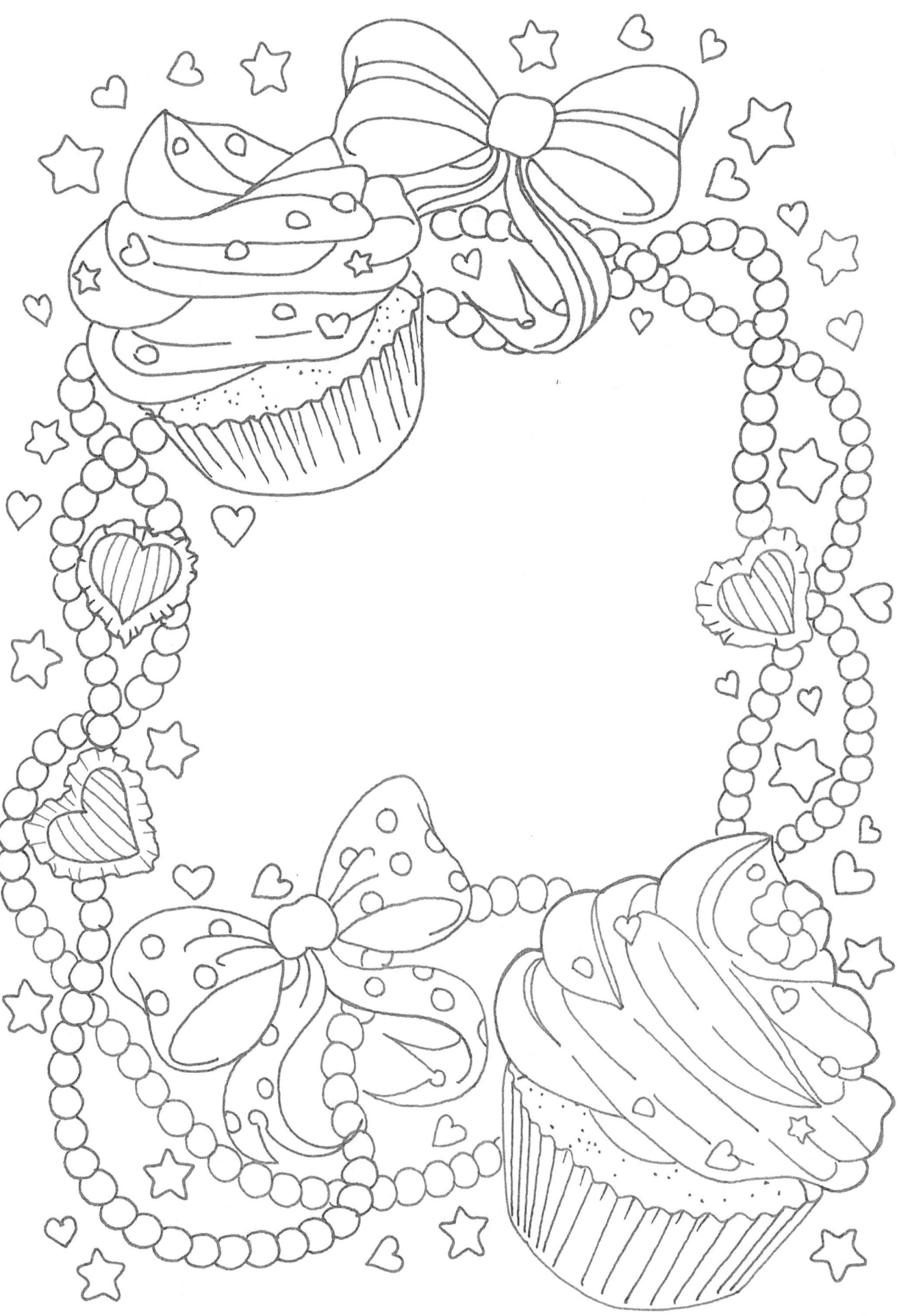

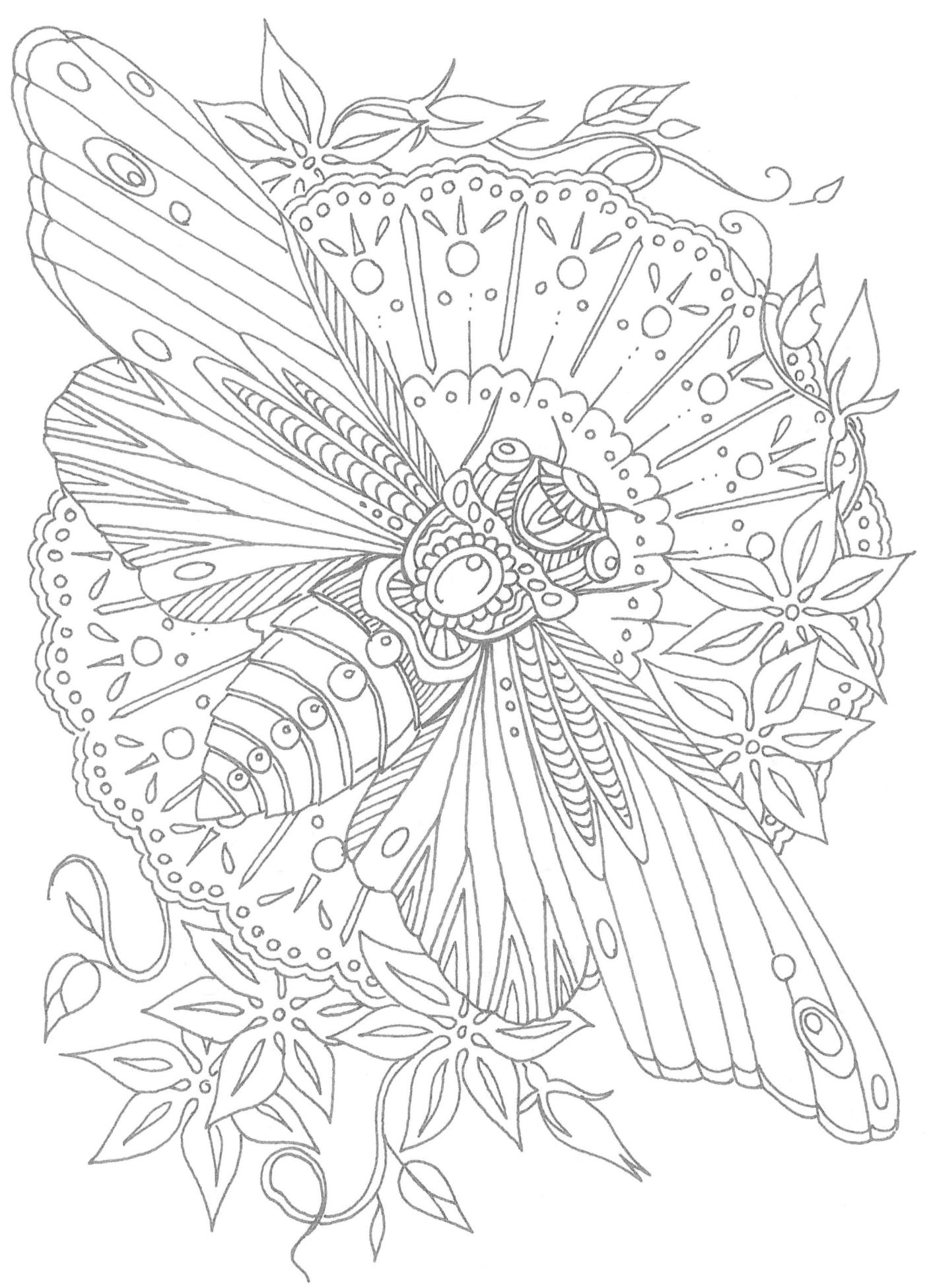

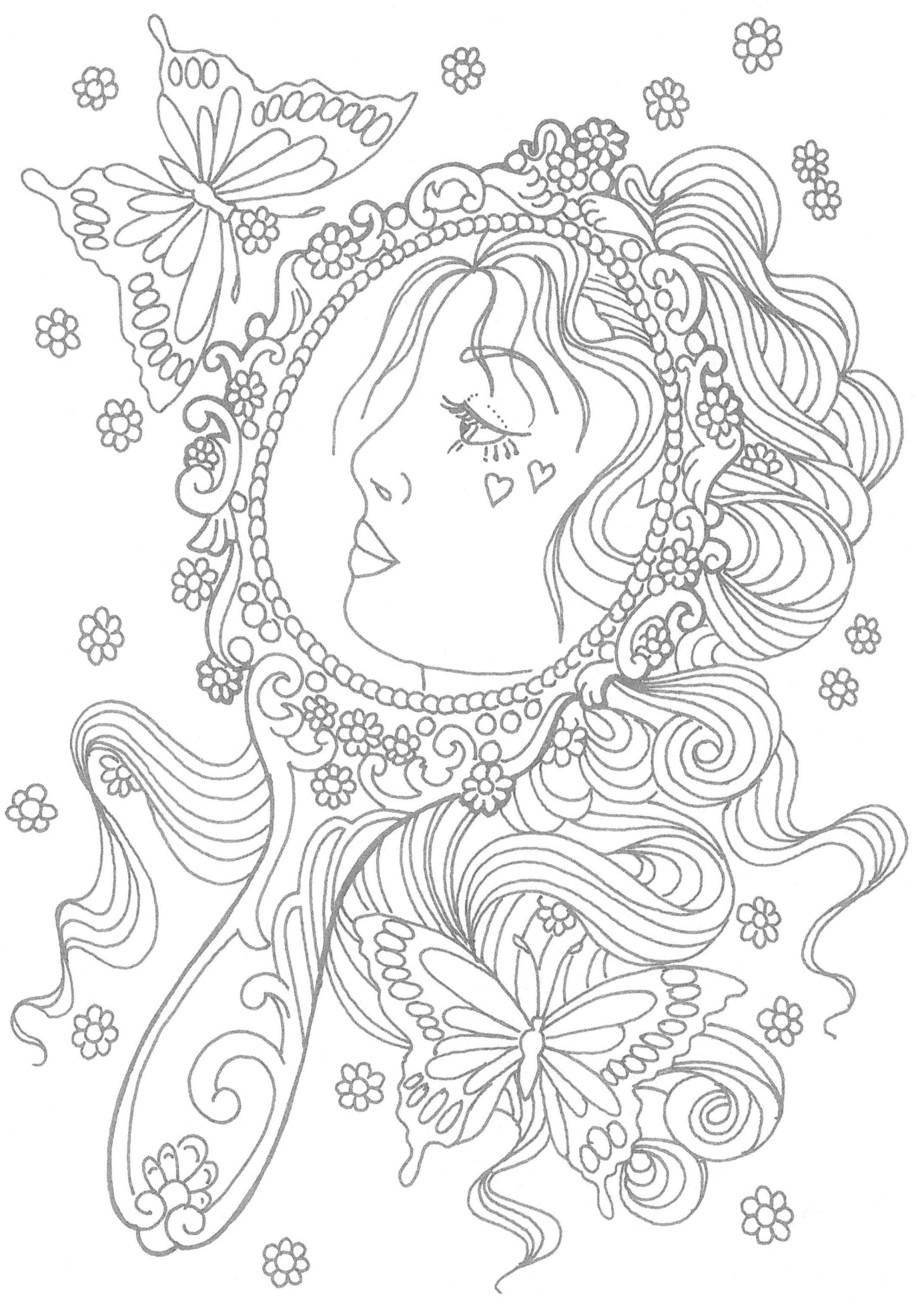

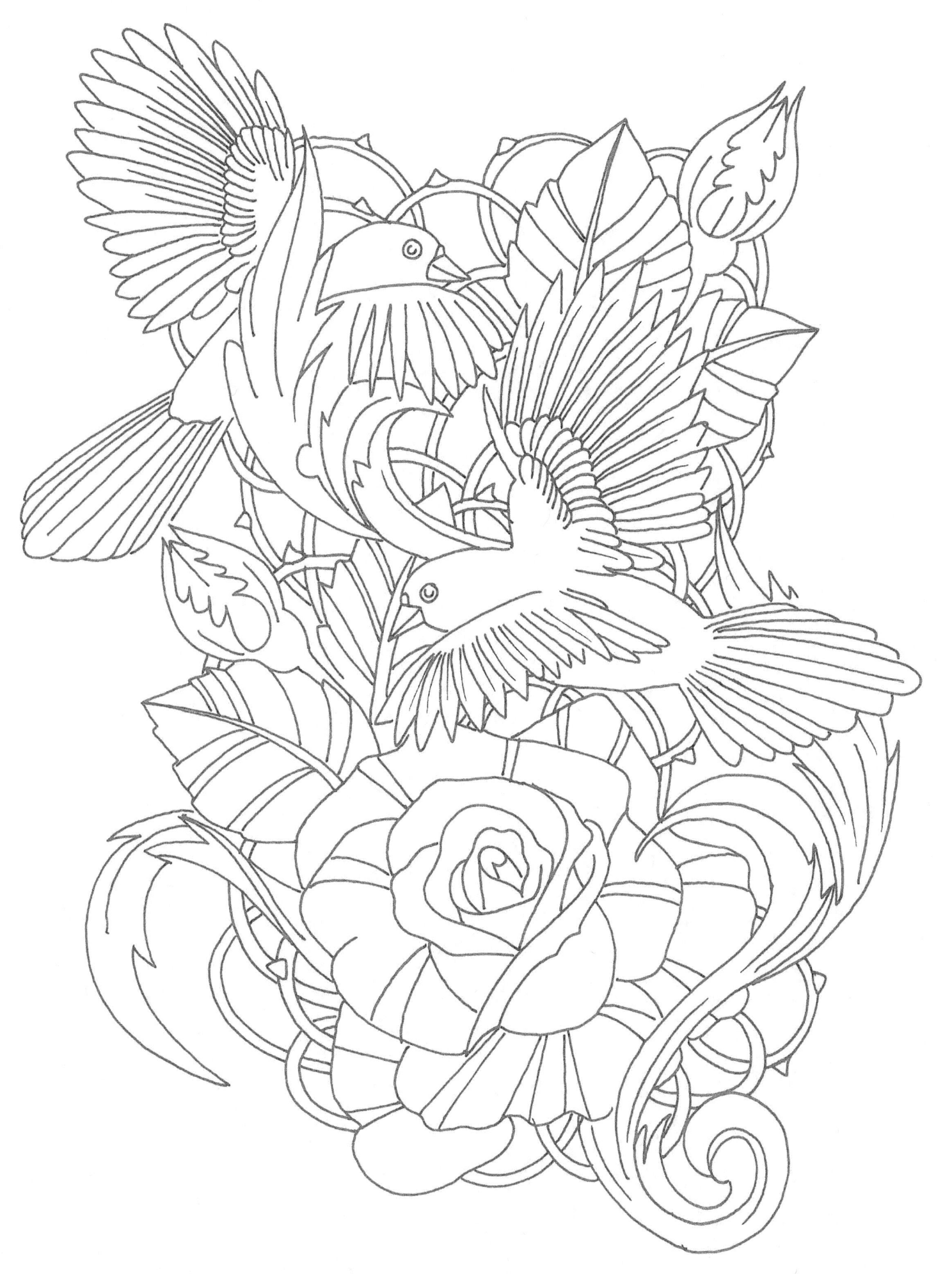

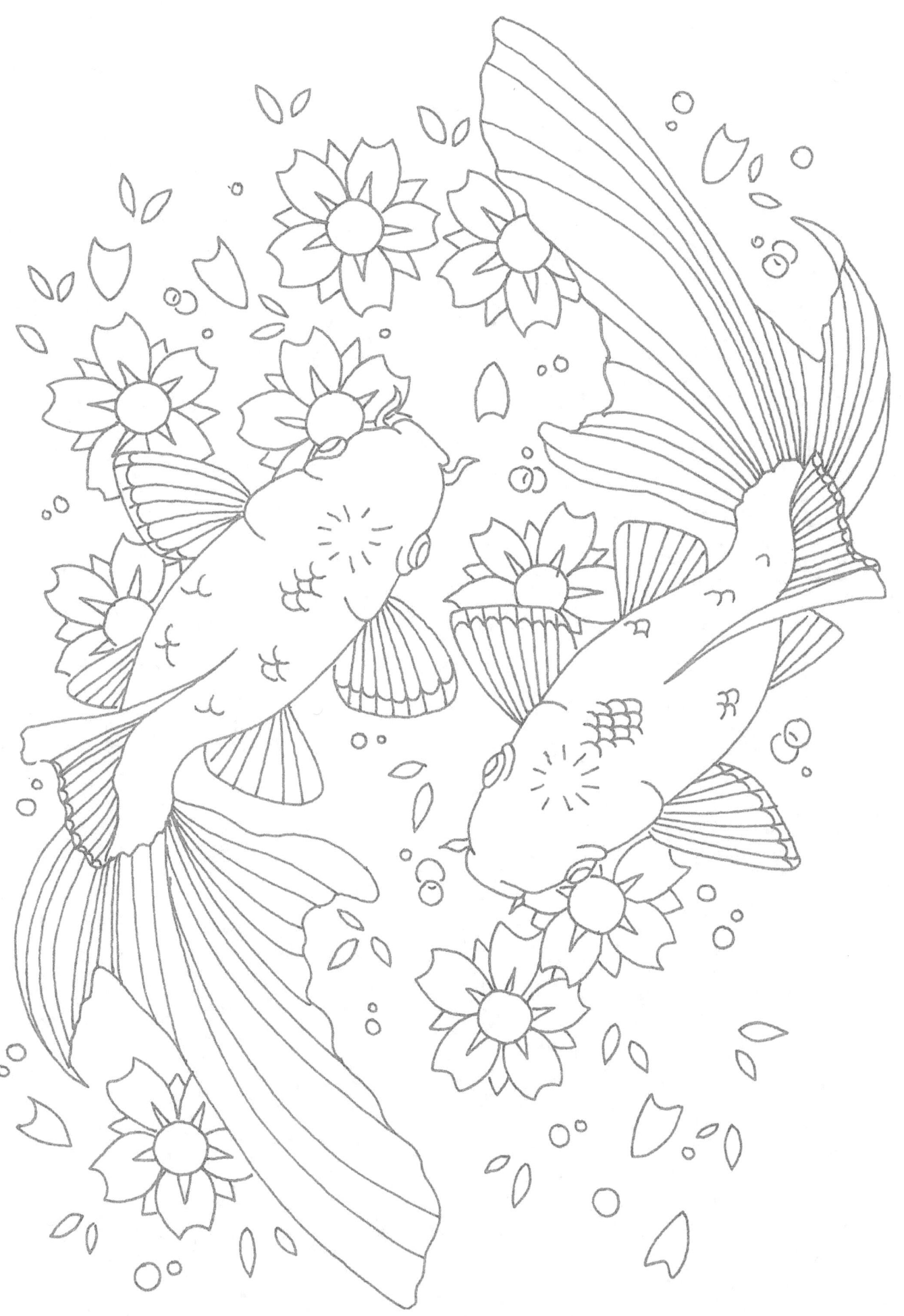

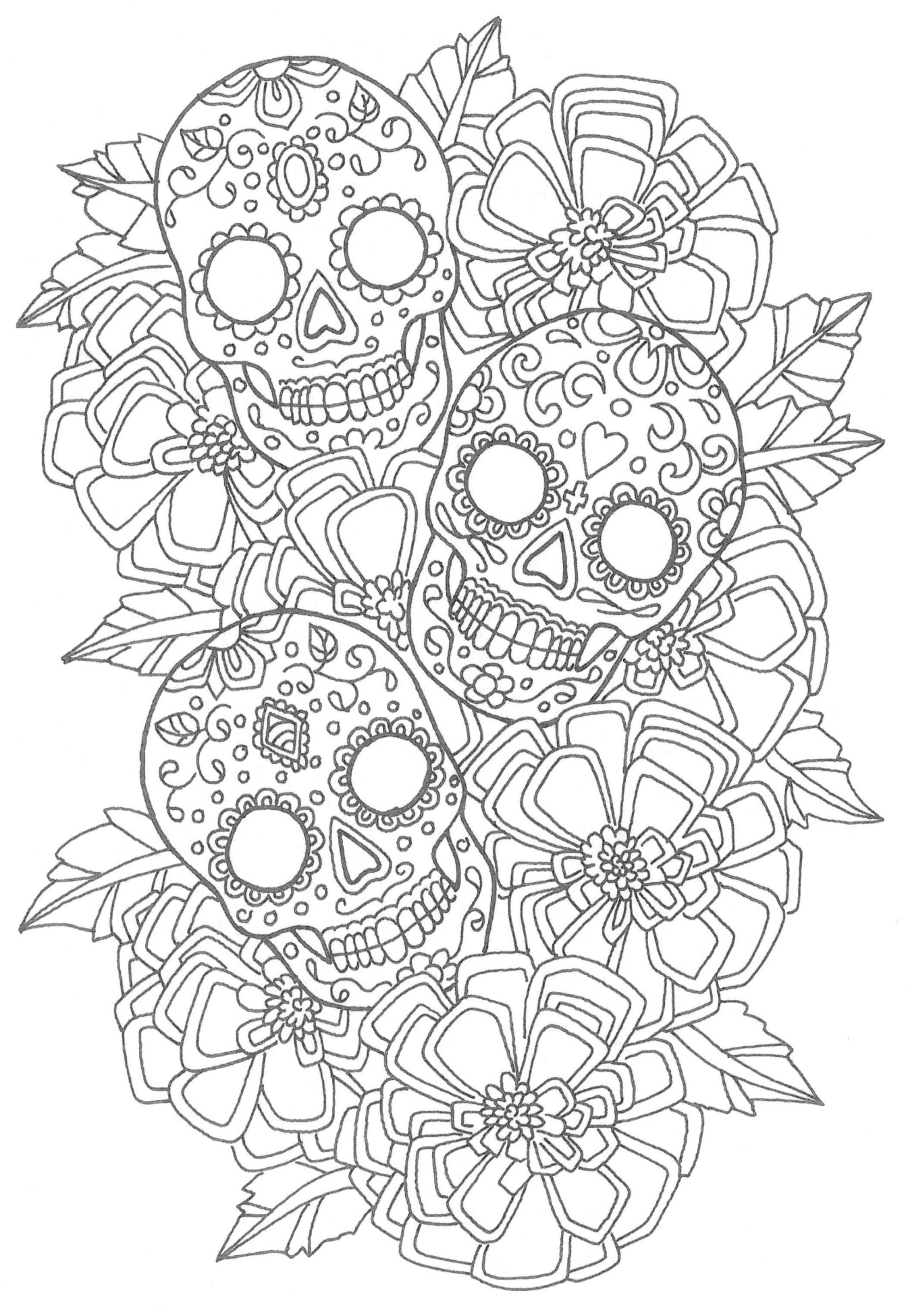

Contributing Artist
Karim Benyagoub
Algeria
Facebook :ZentangleArt0626

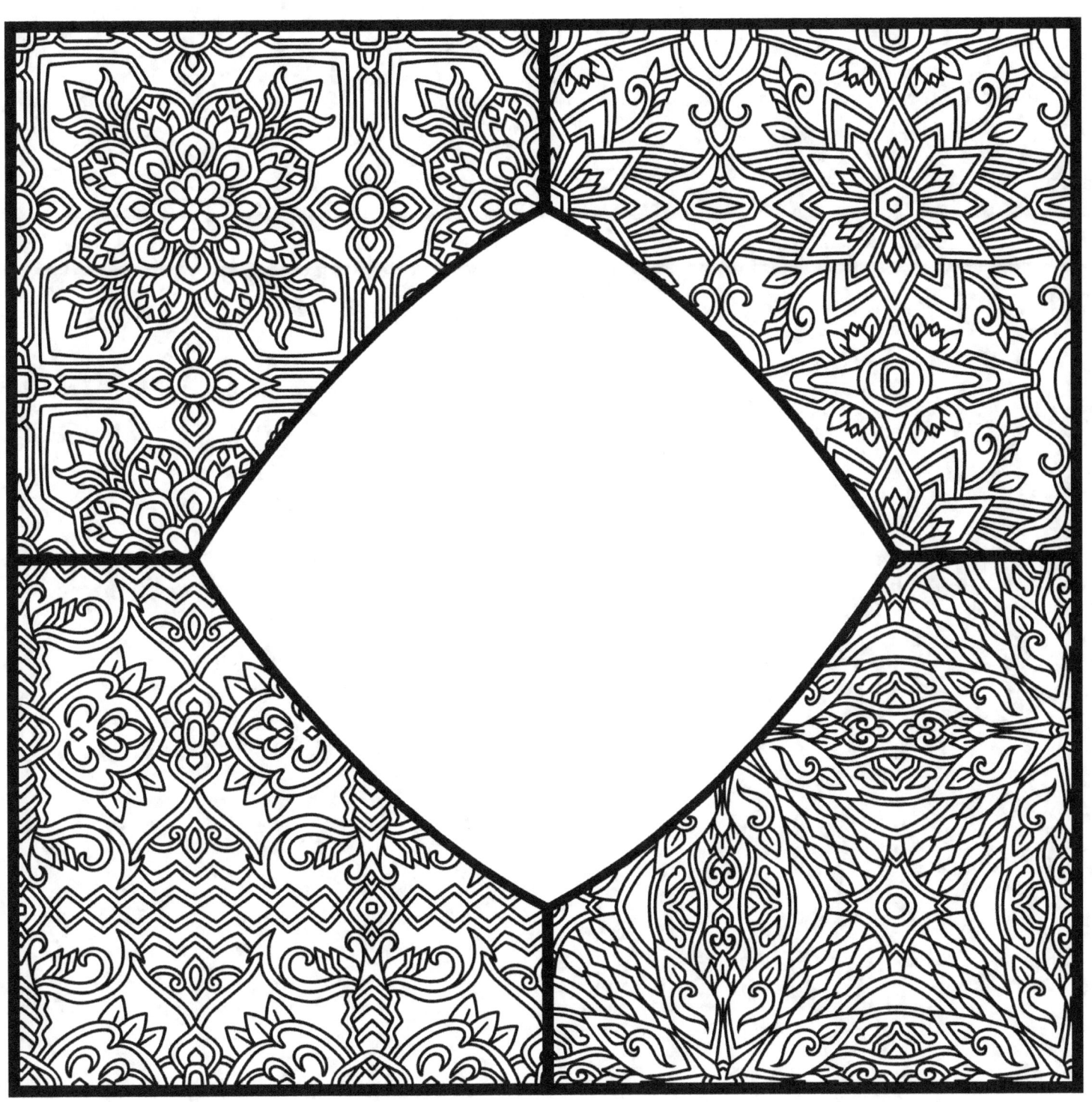

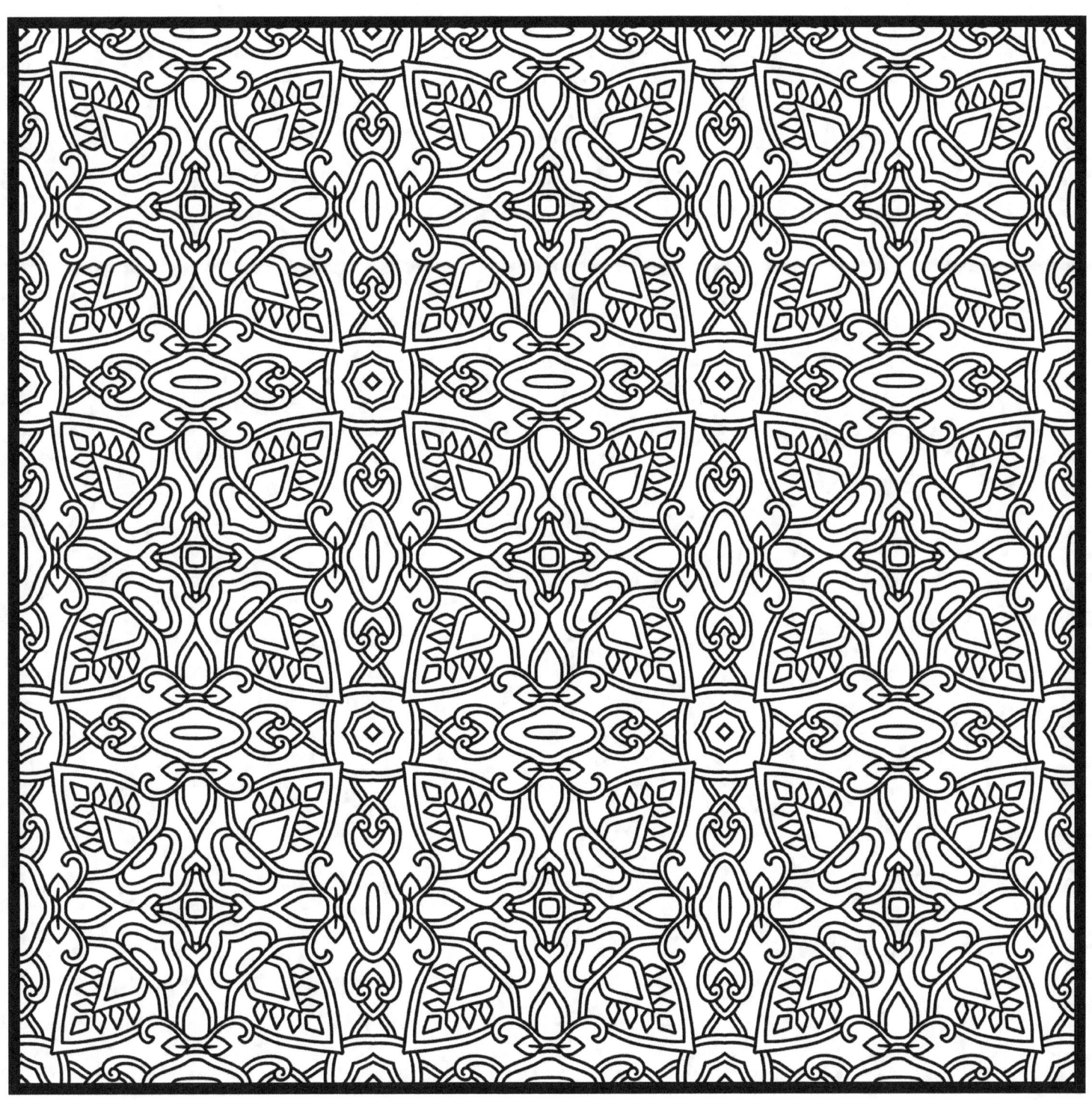

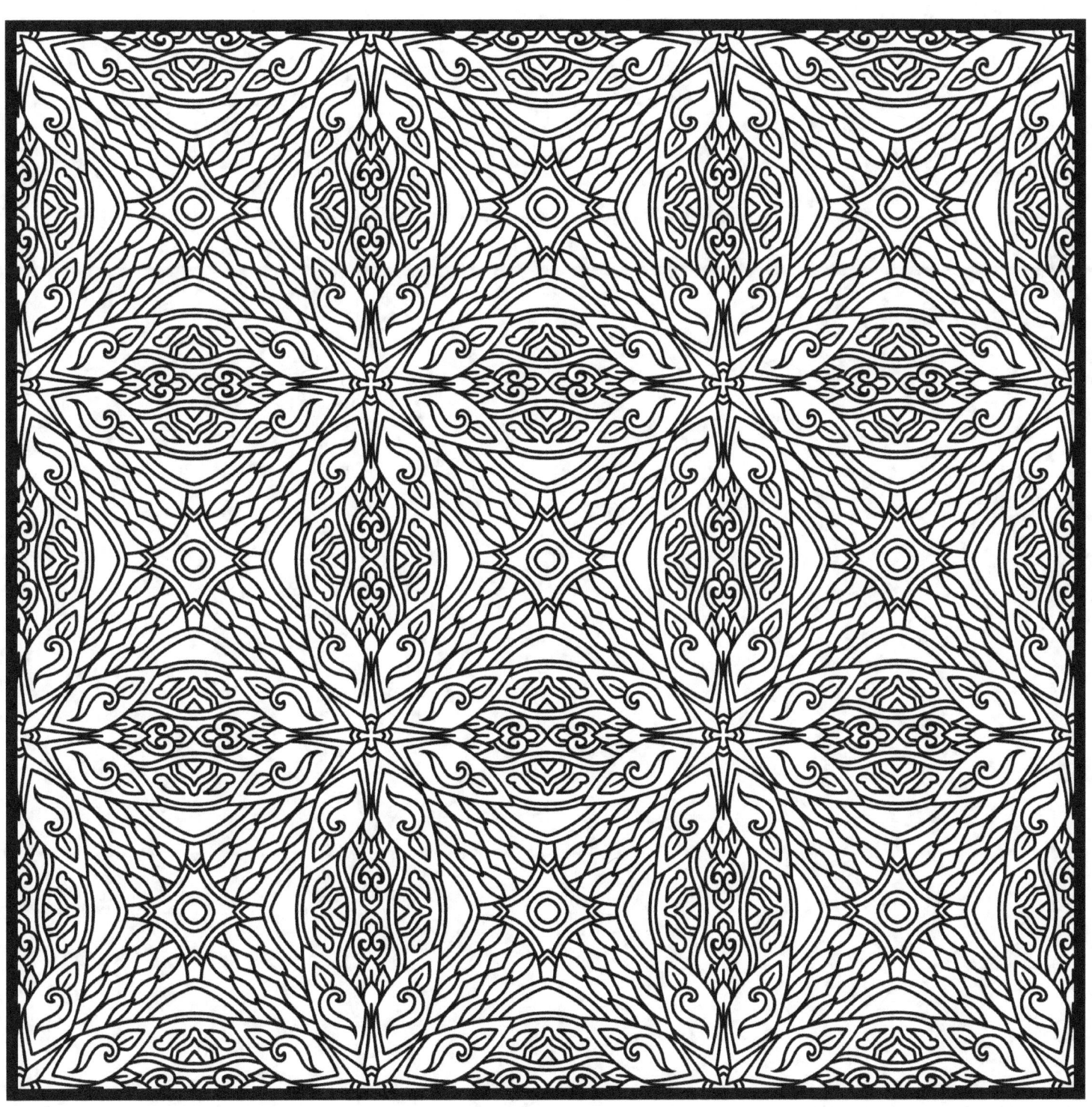

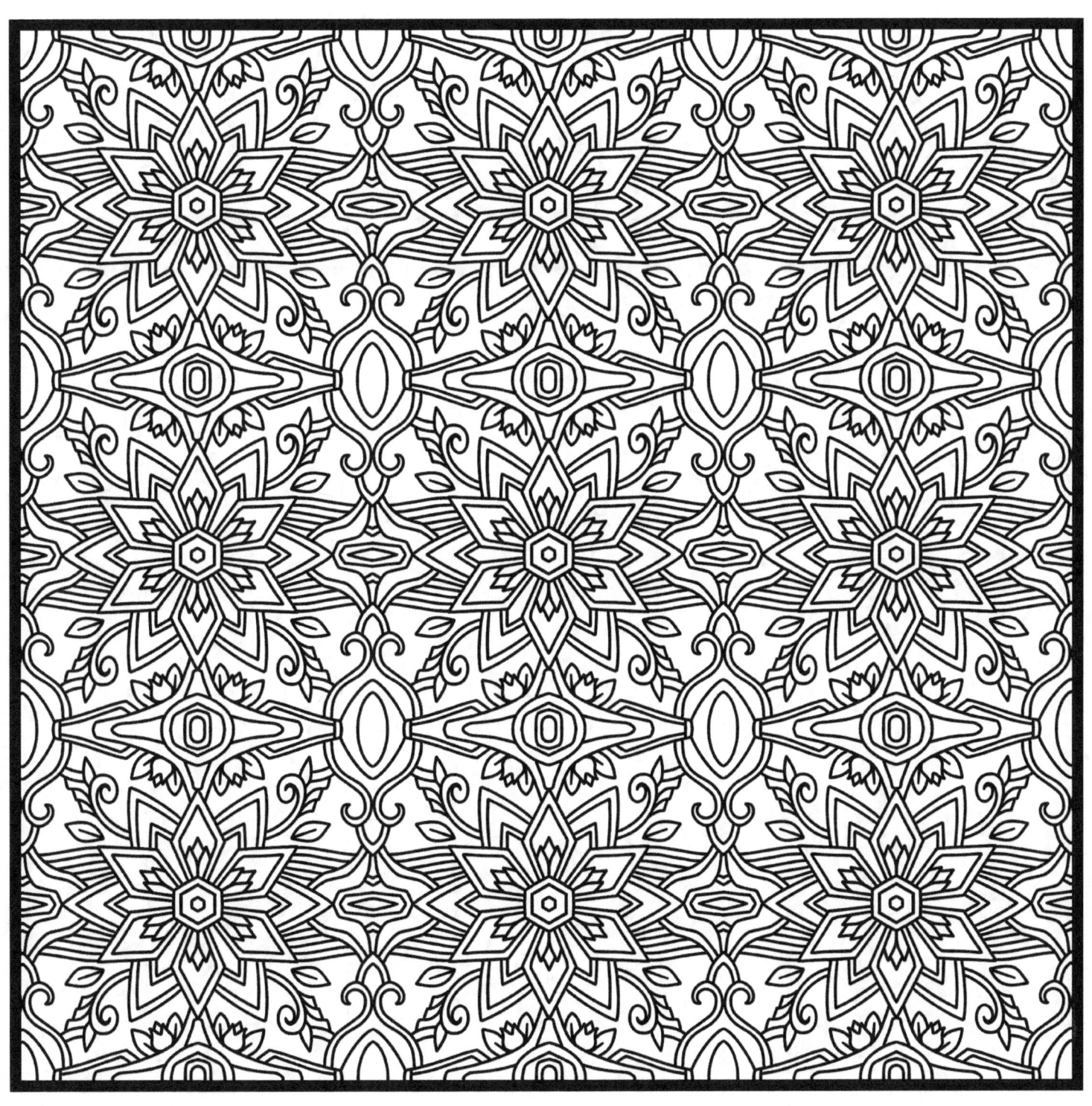

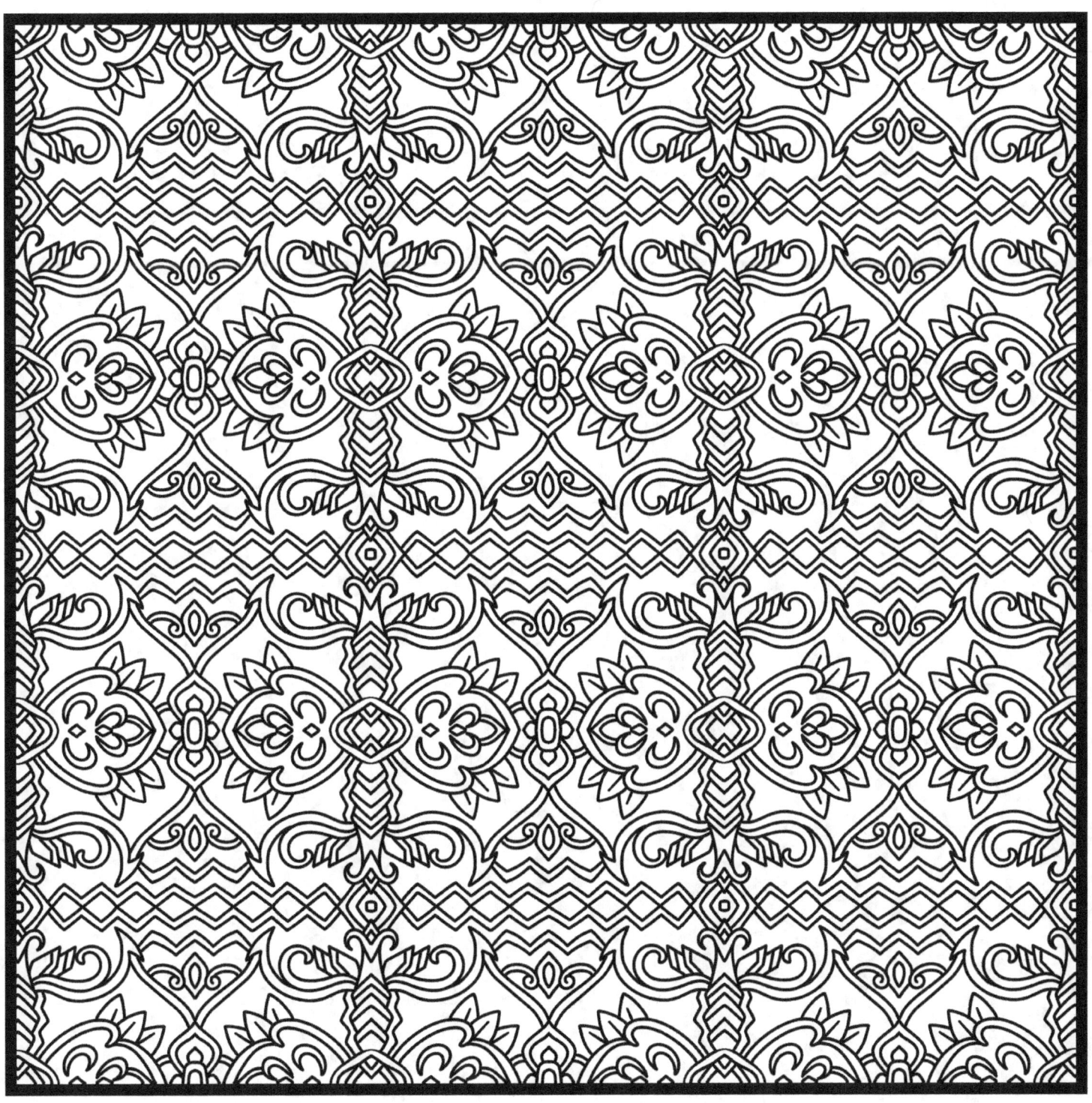

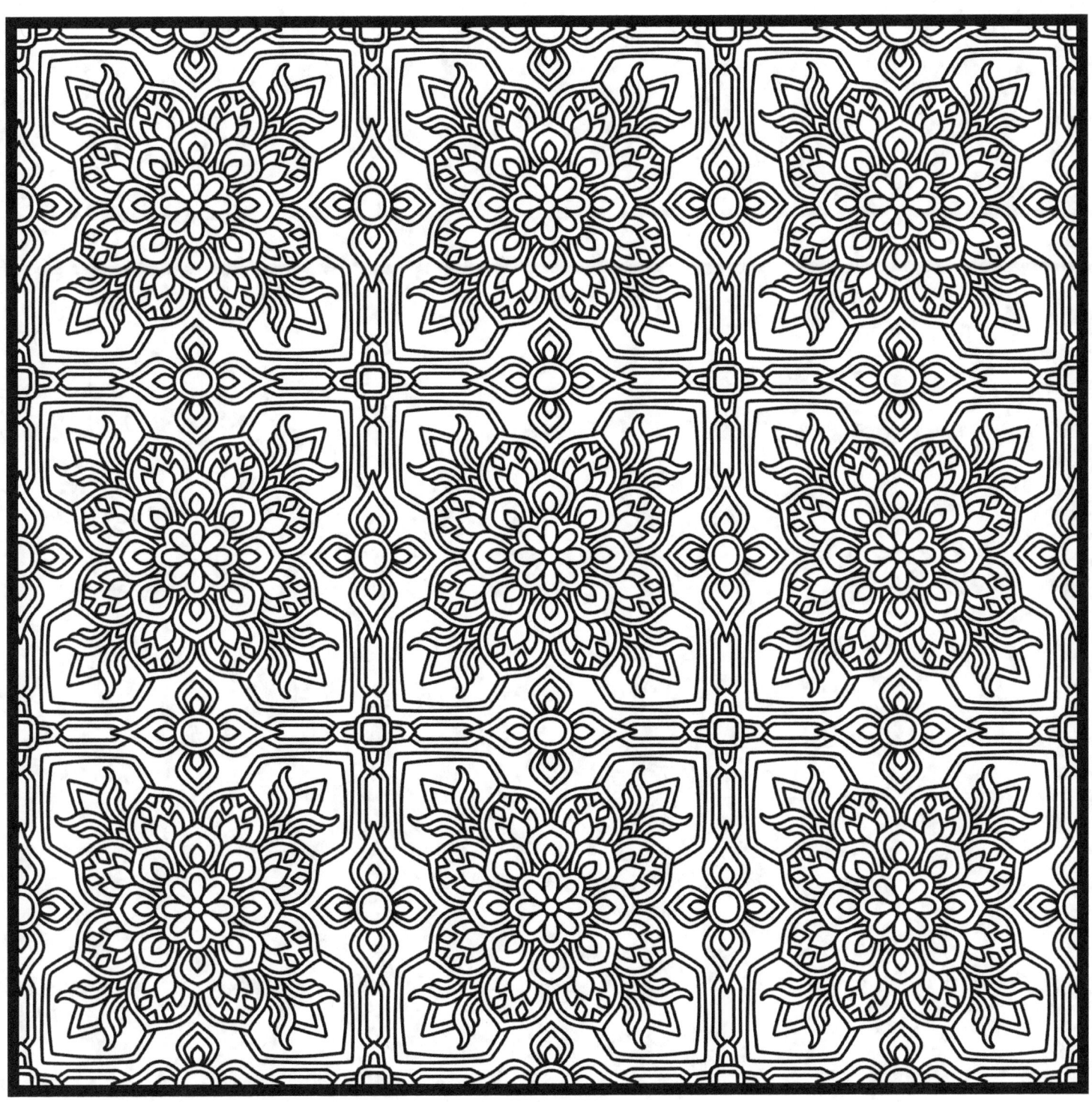

Contributing Artist
Jenny Wei
Taiwan

Facebook : zentangle fun

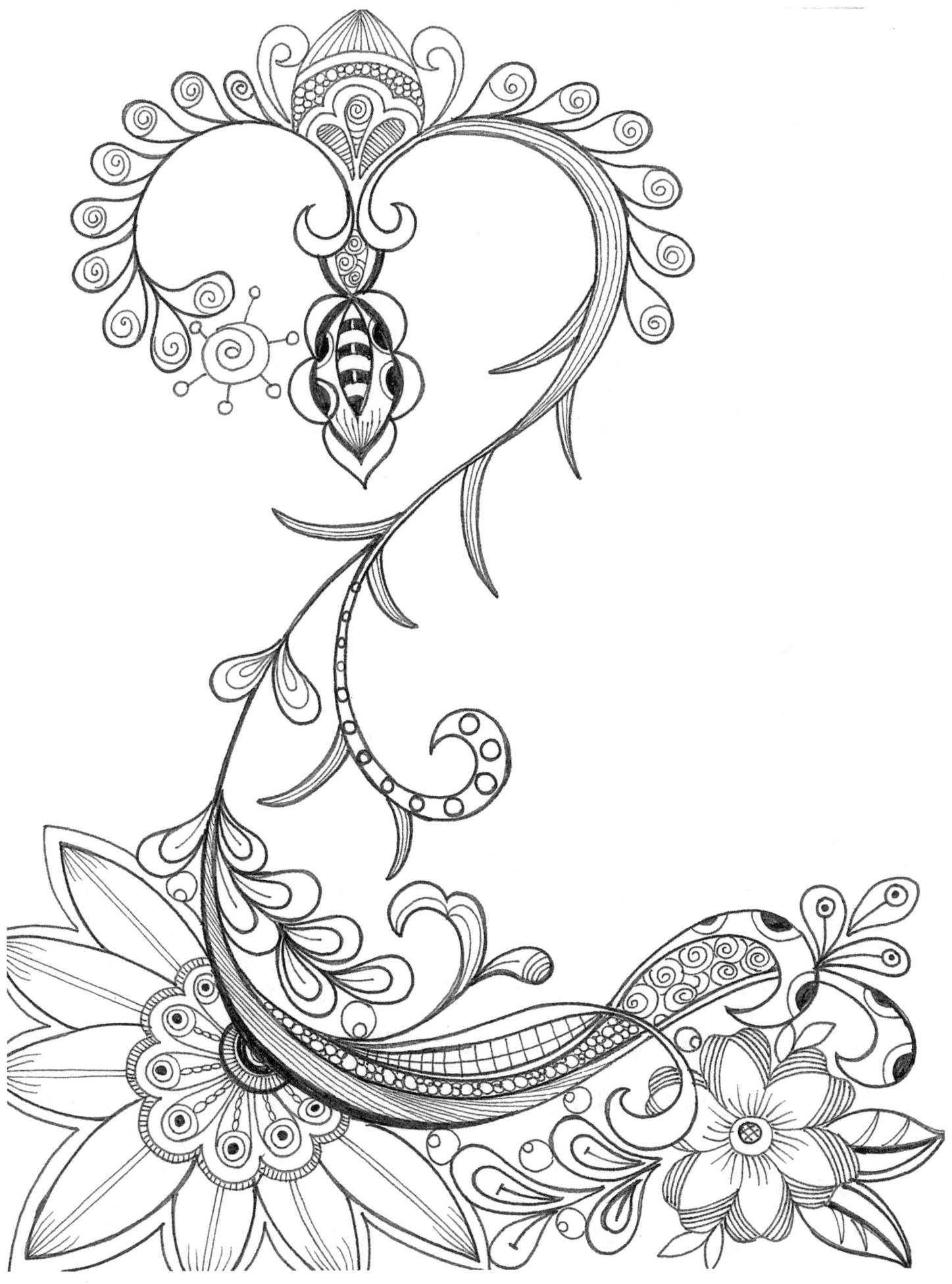

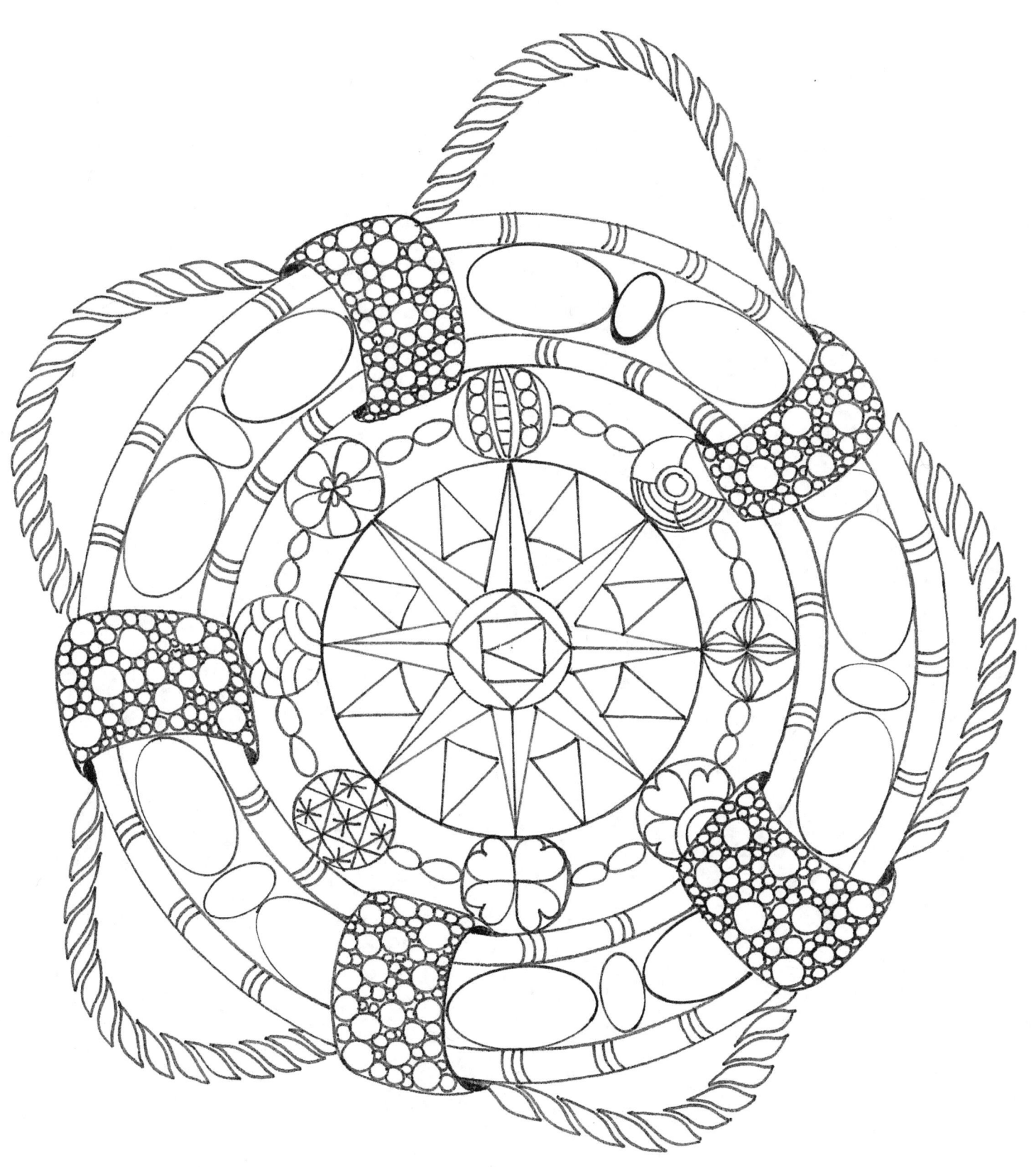

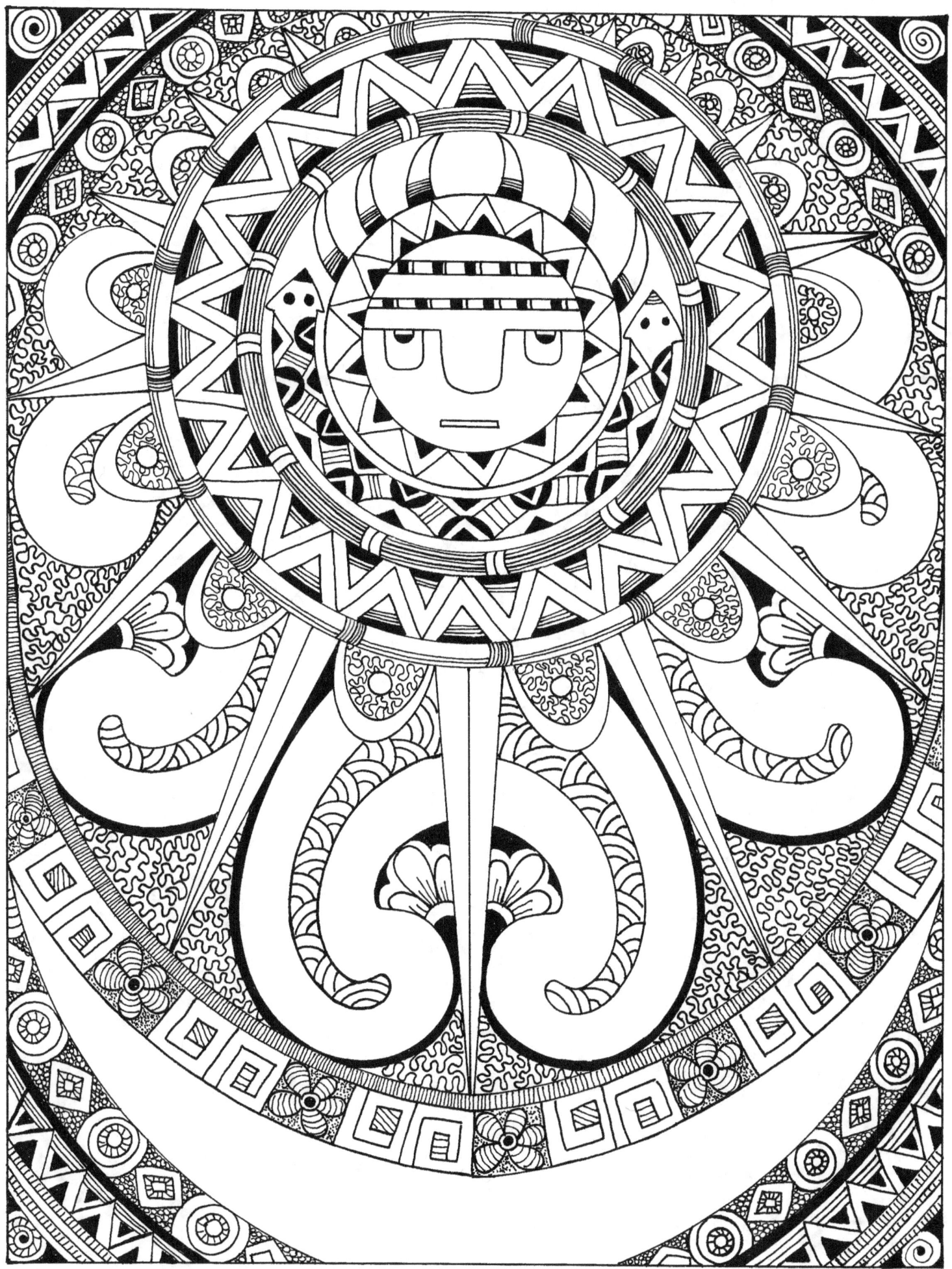

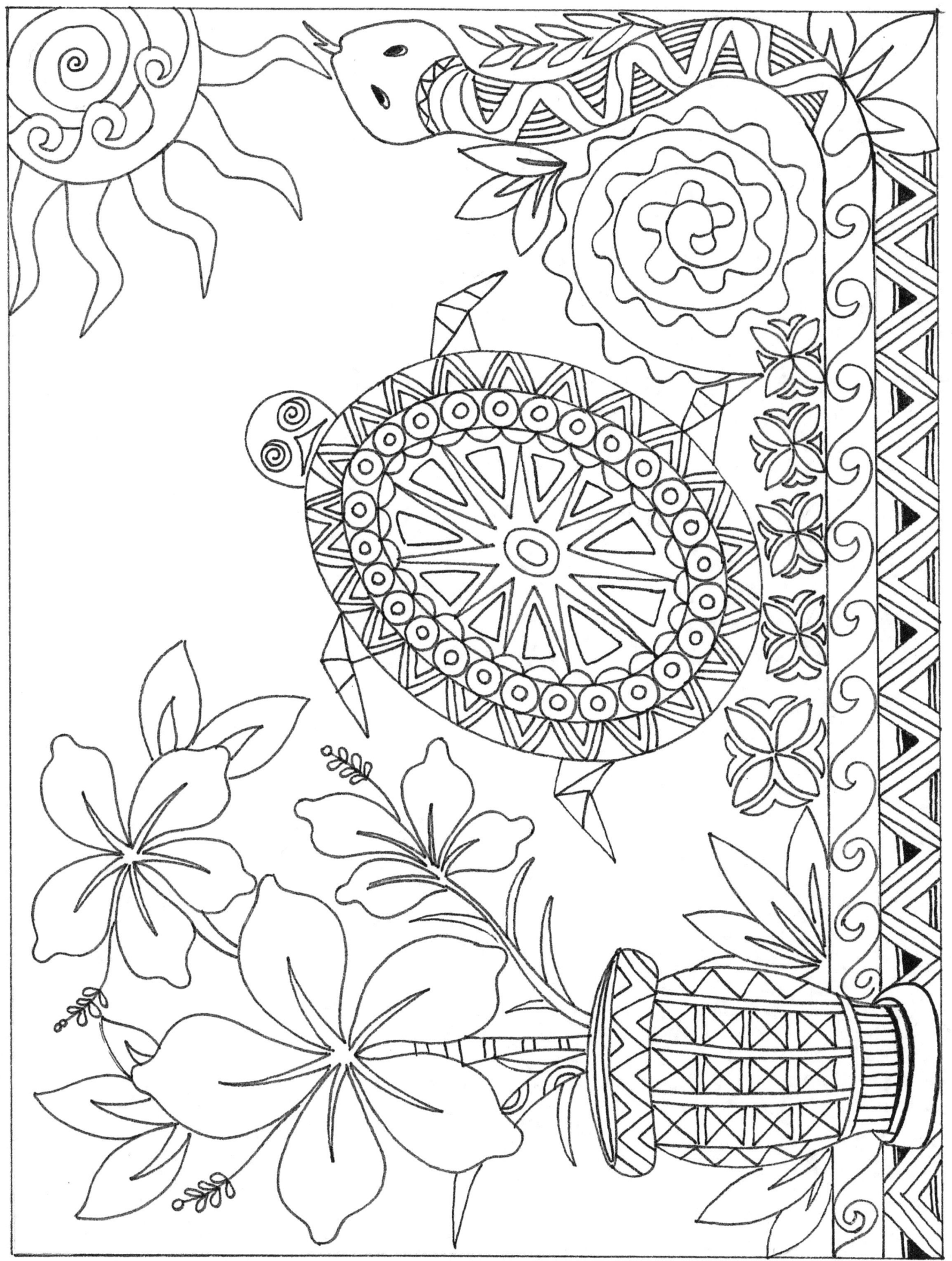

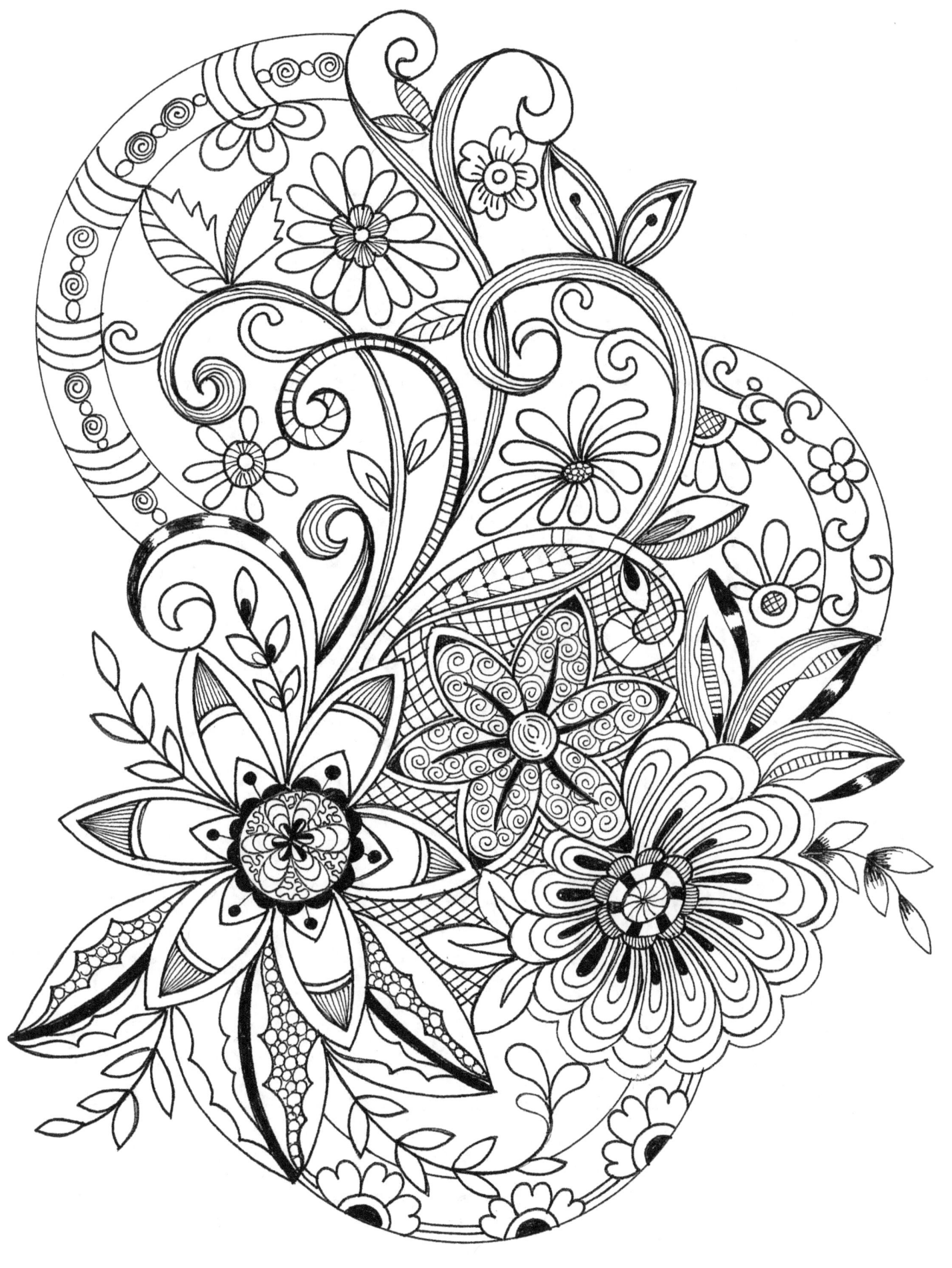

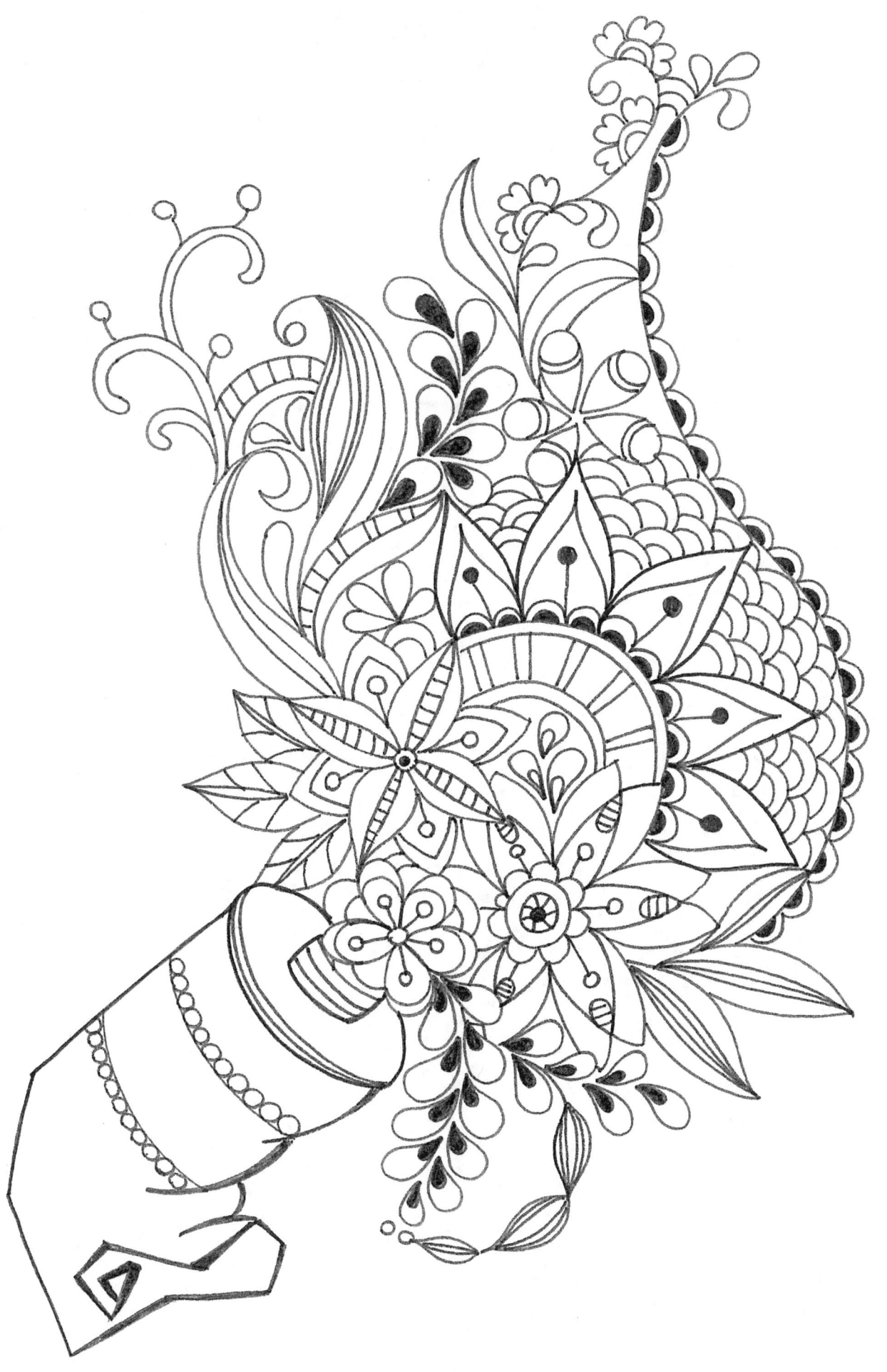

Contributing Artist
Andrea Sargent
USA

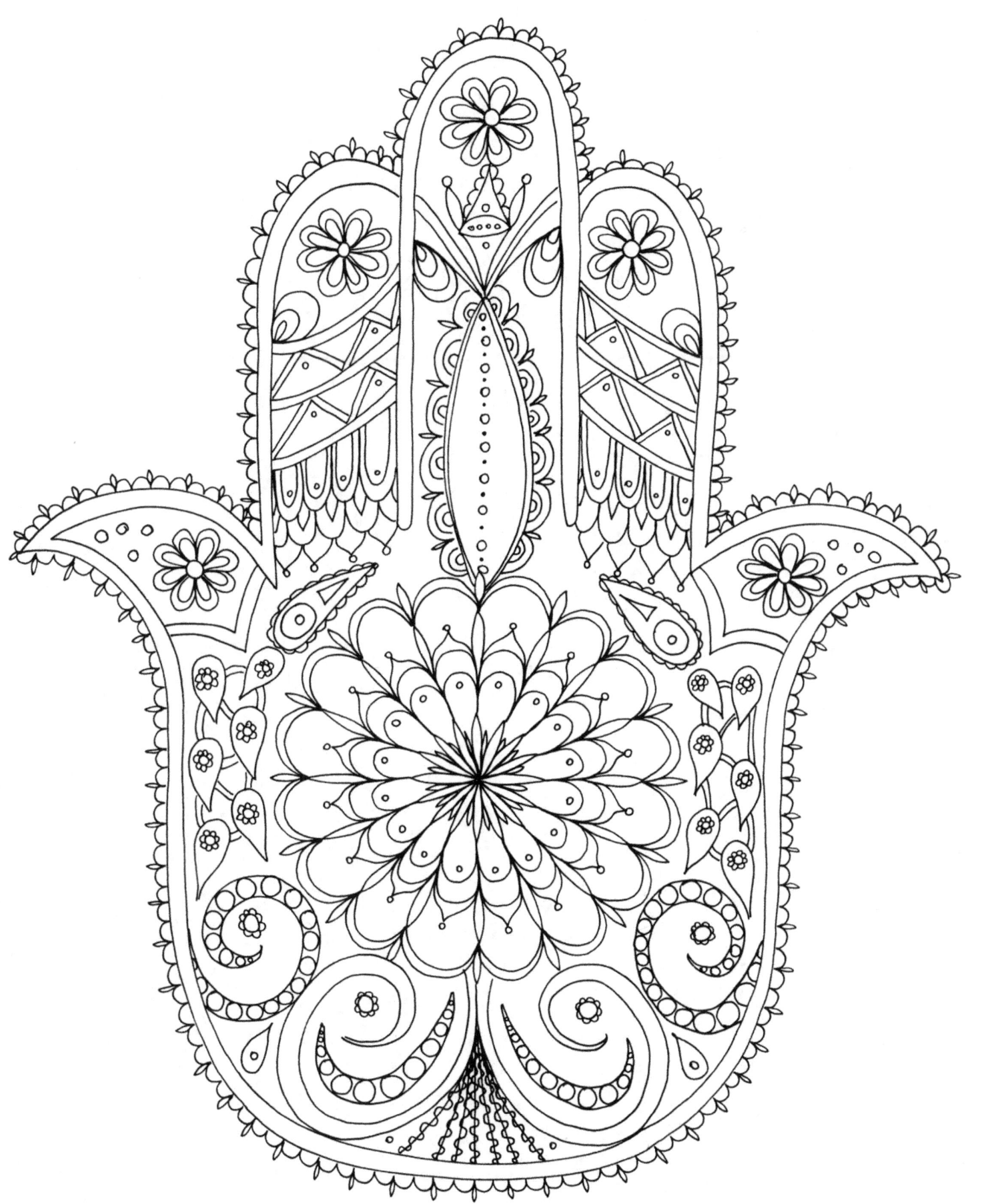

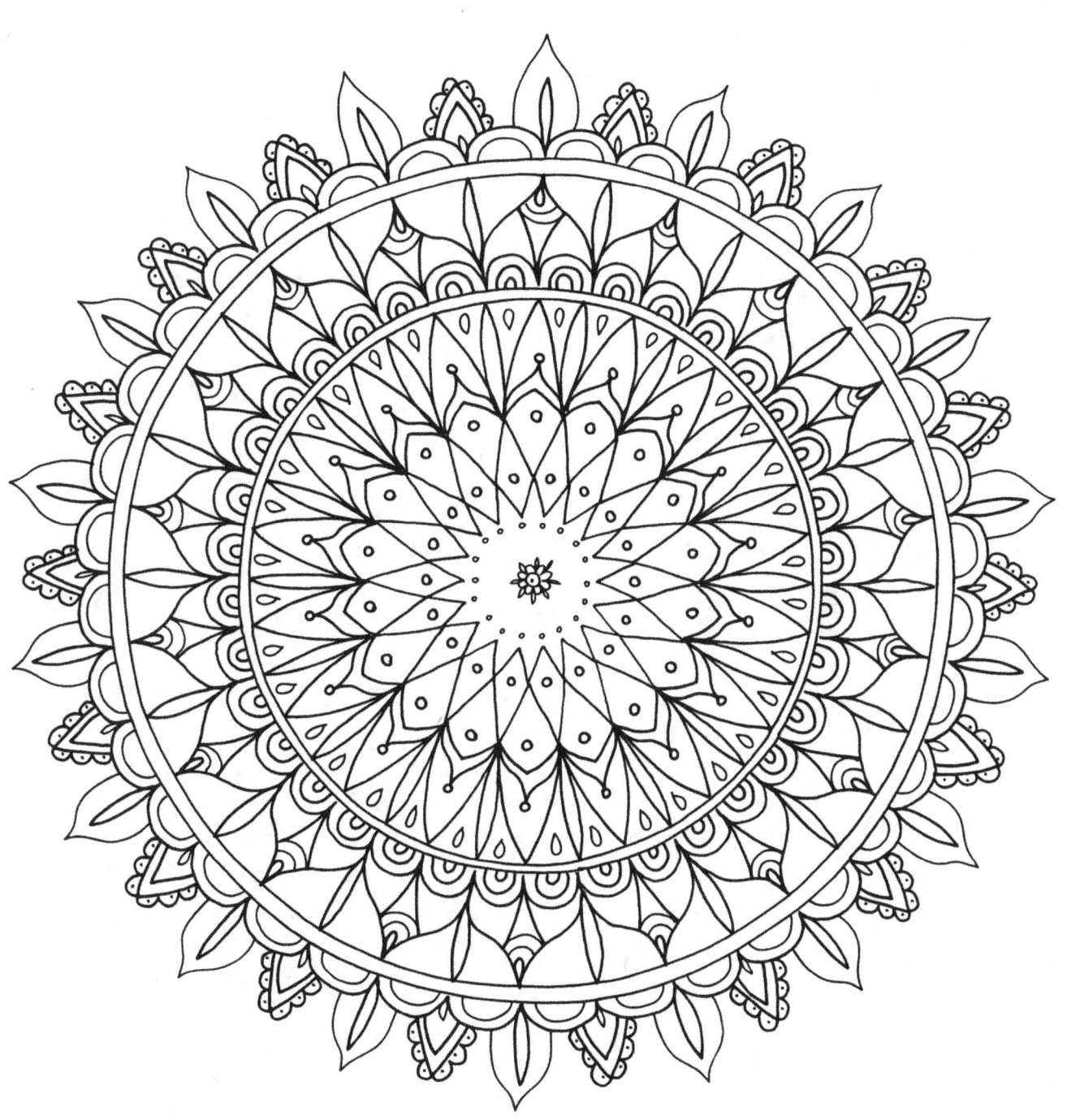

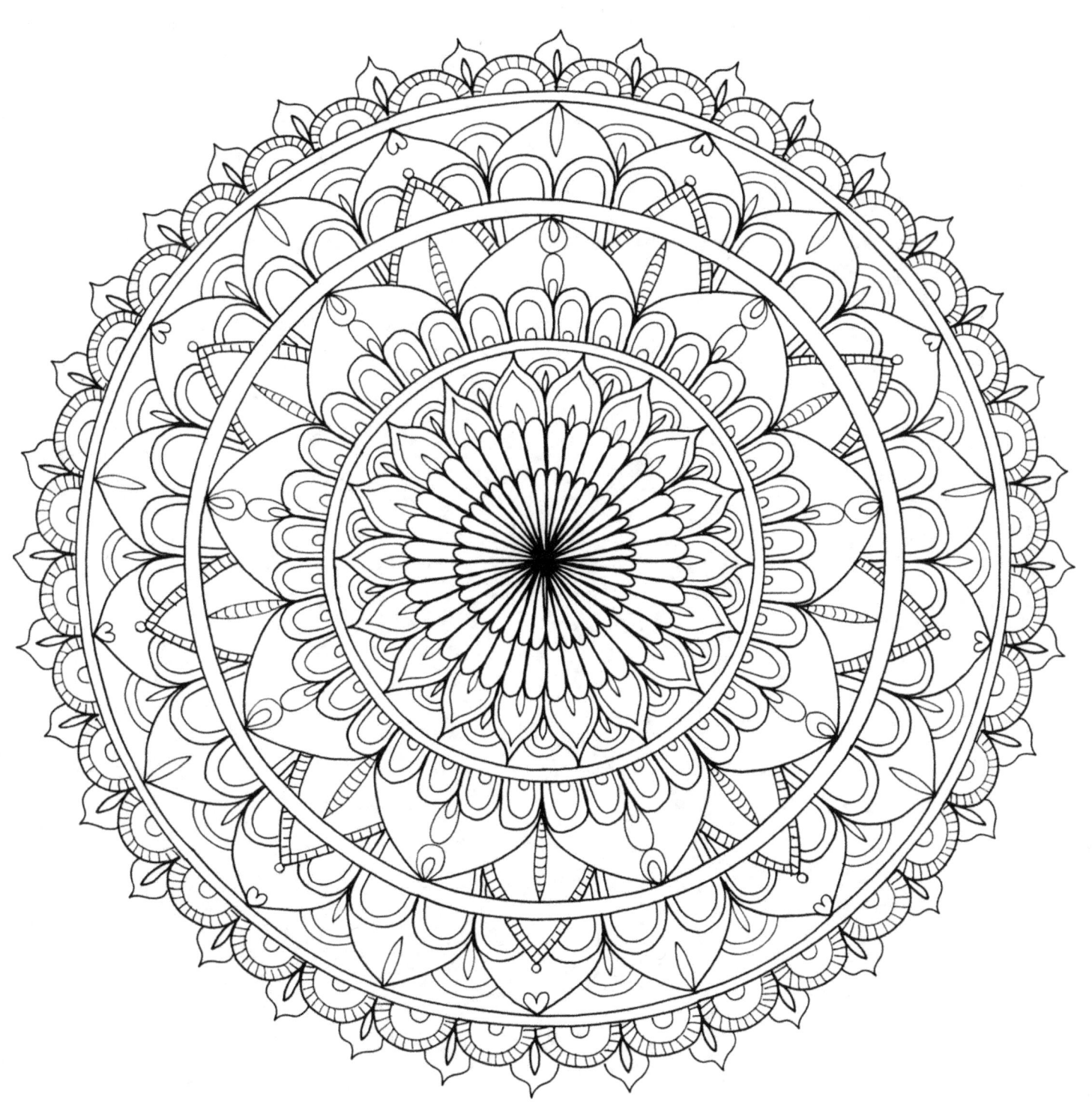

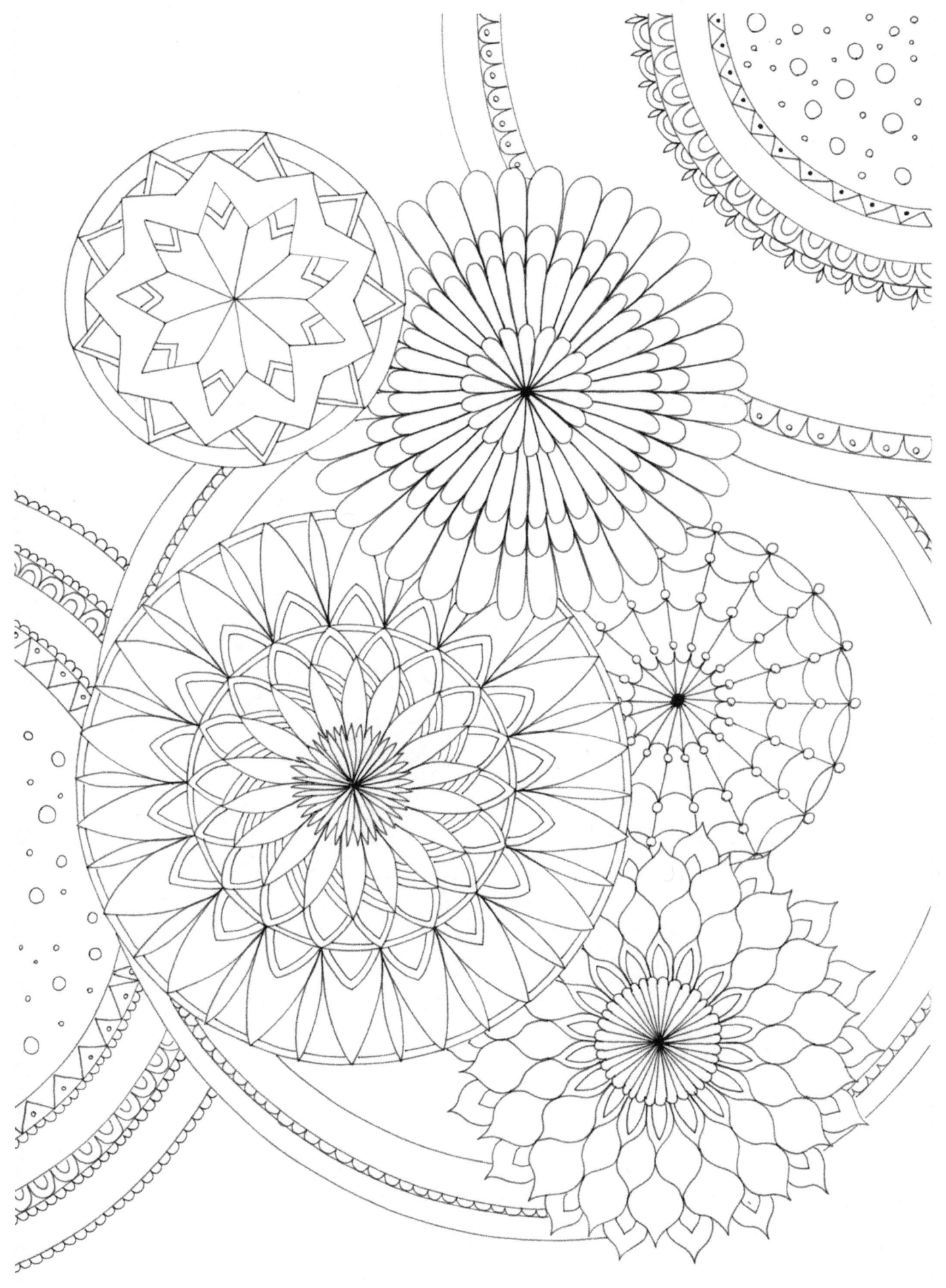

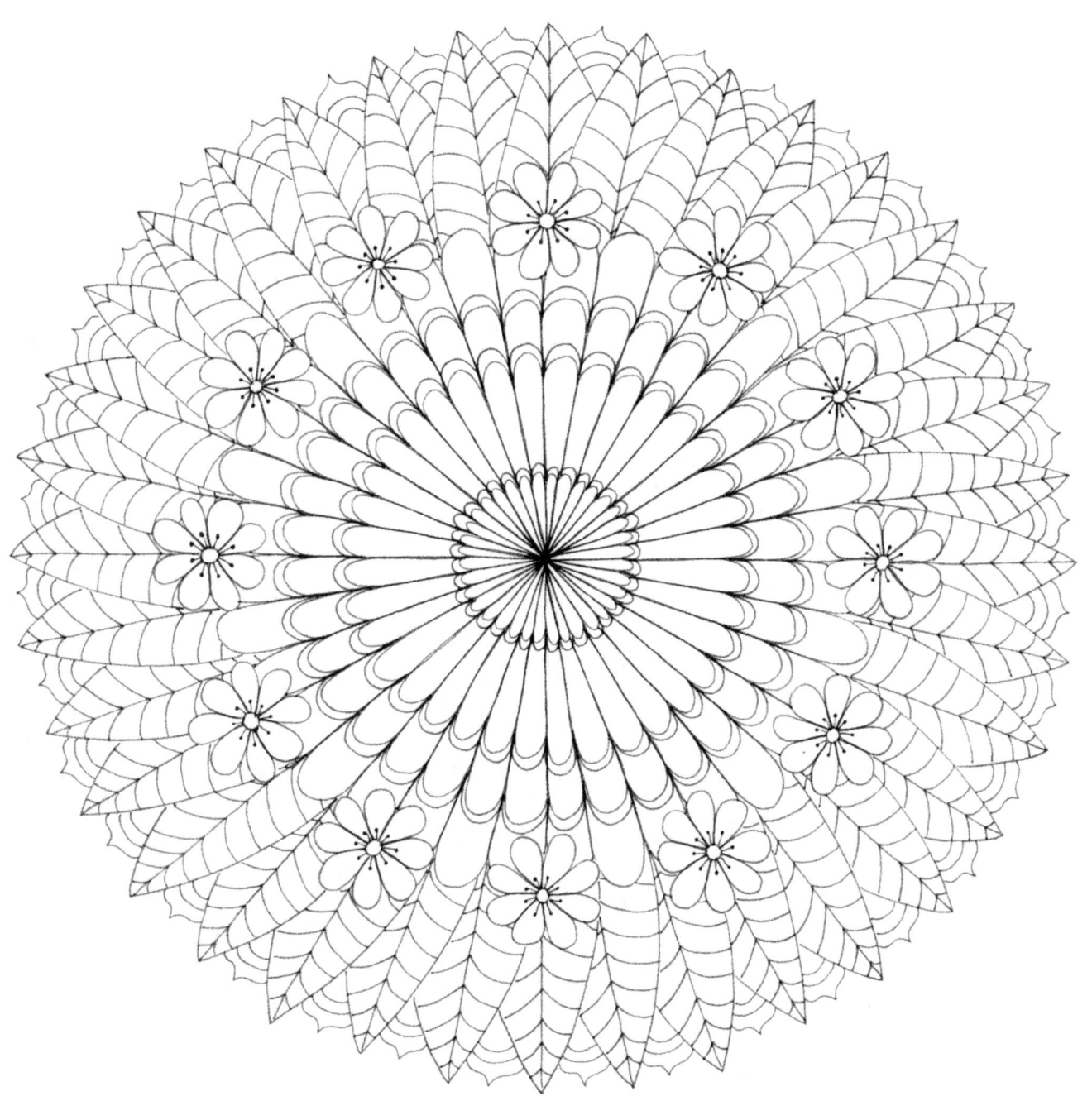

Contributing Artist
Wanting Huang
Taiwan

Facebook : Raccoon's Countryside Illustration

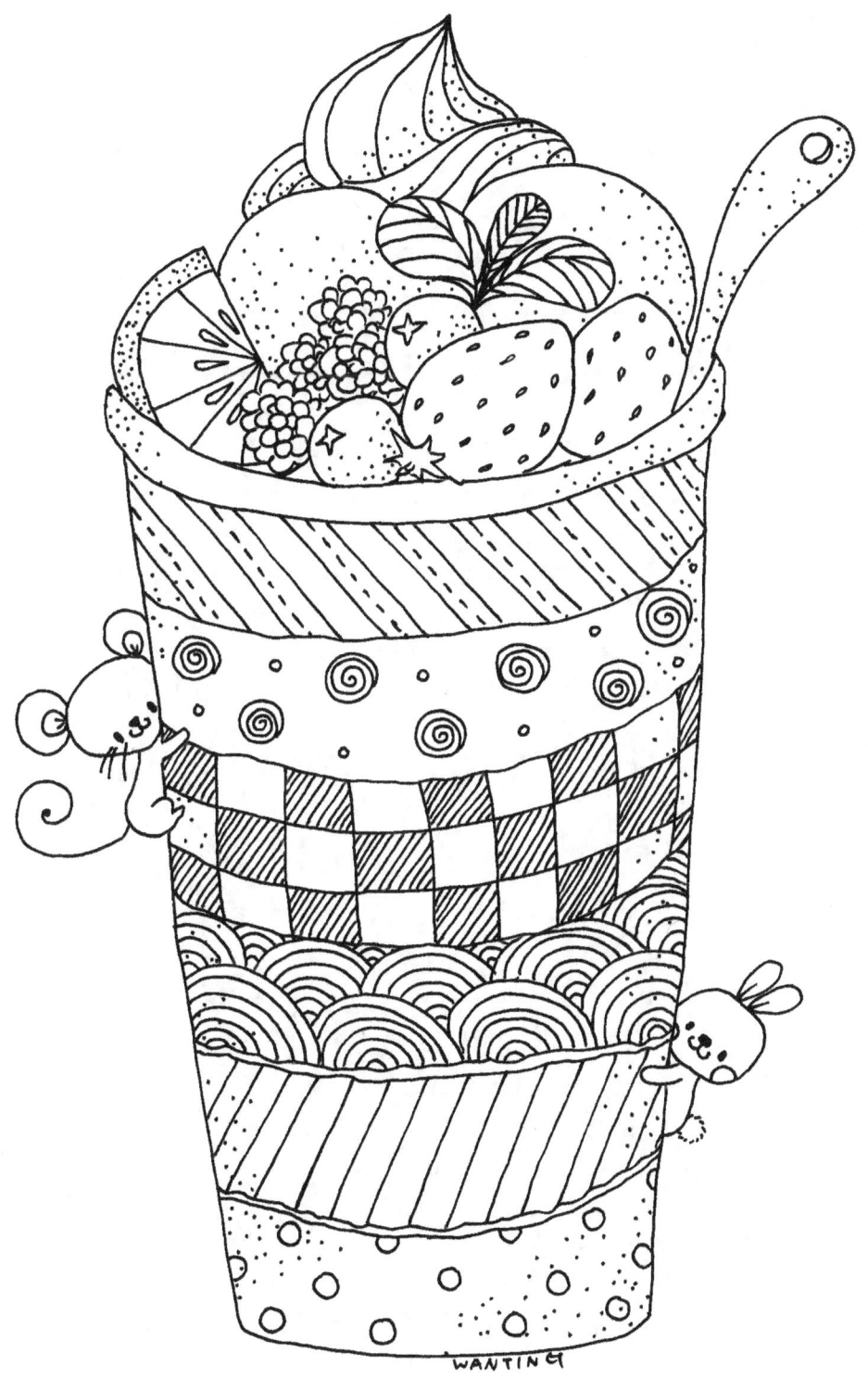

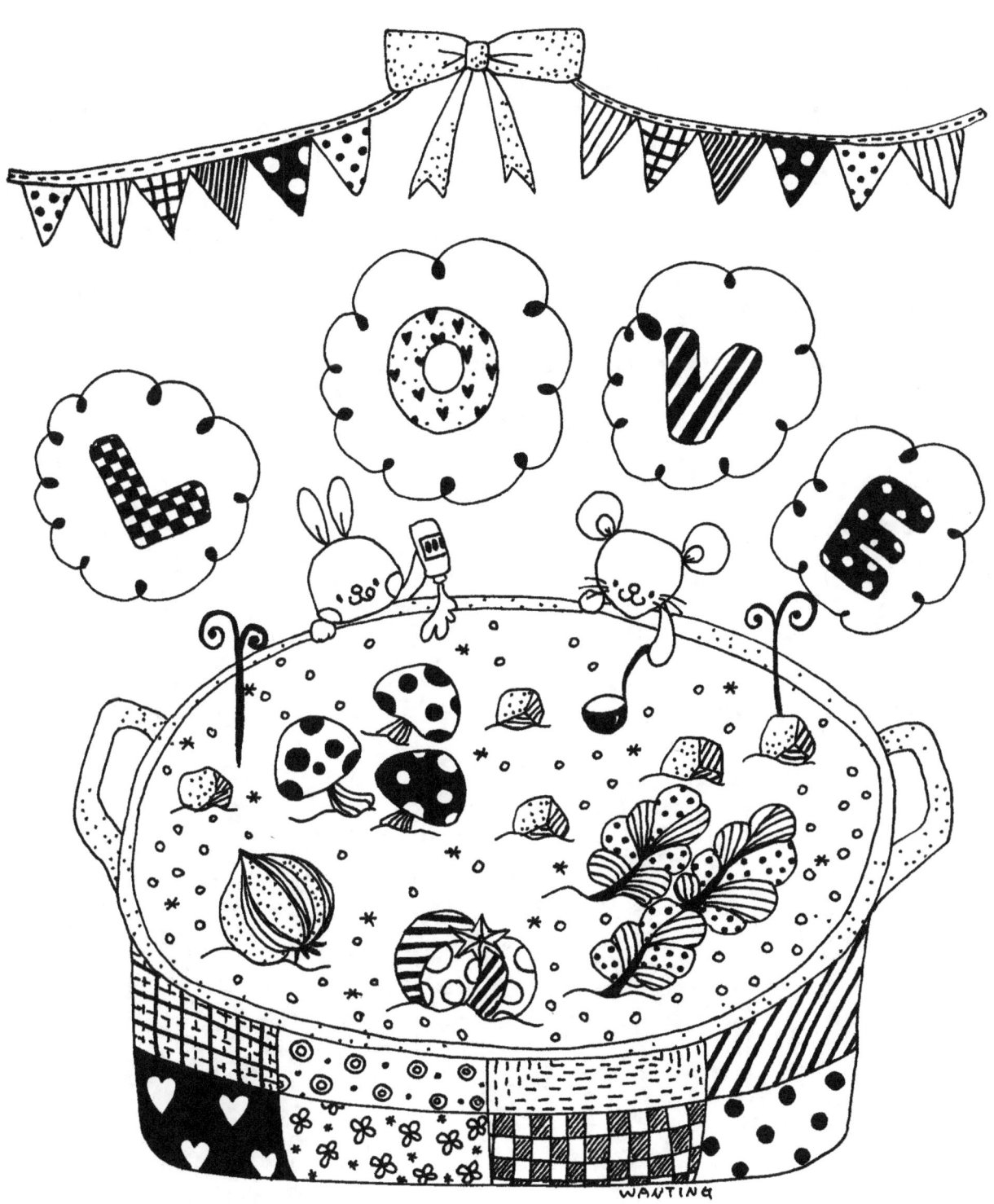

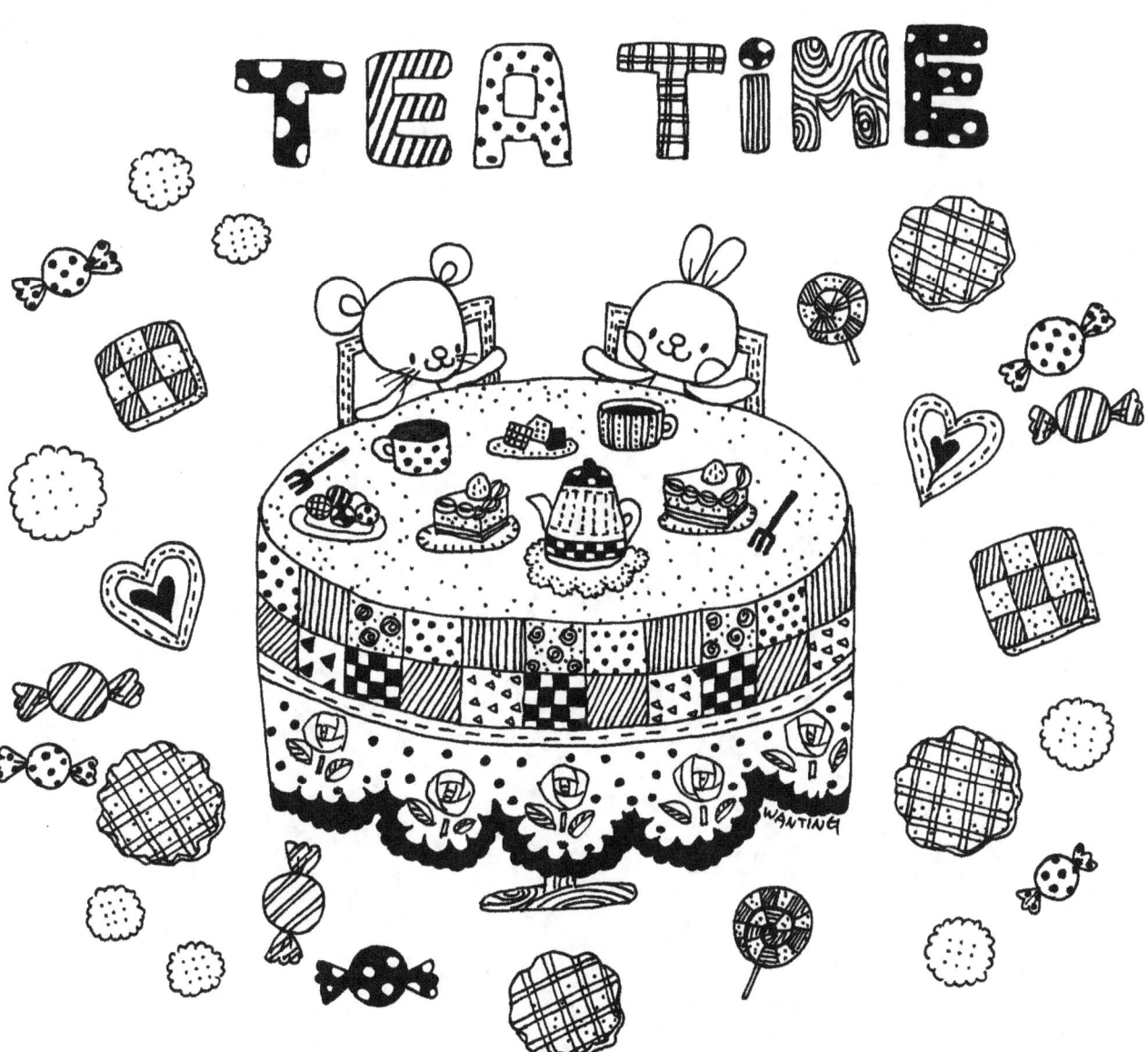

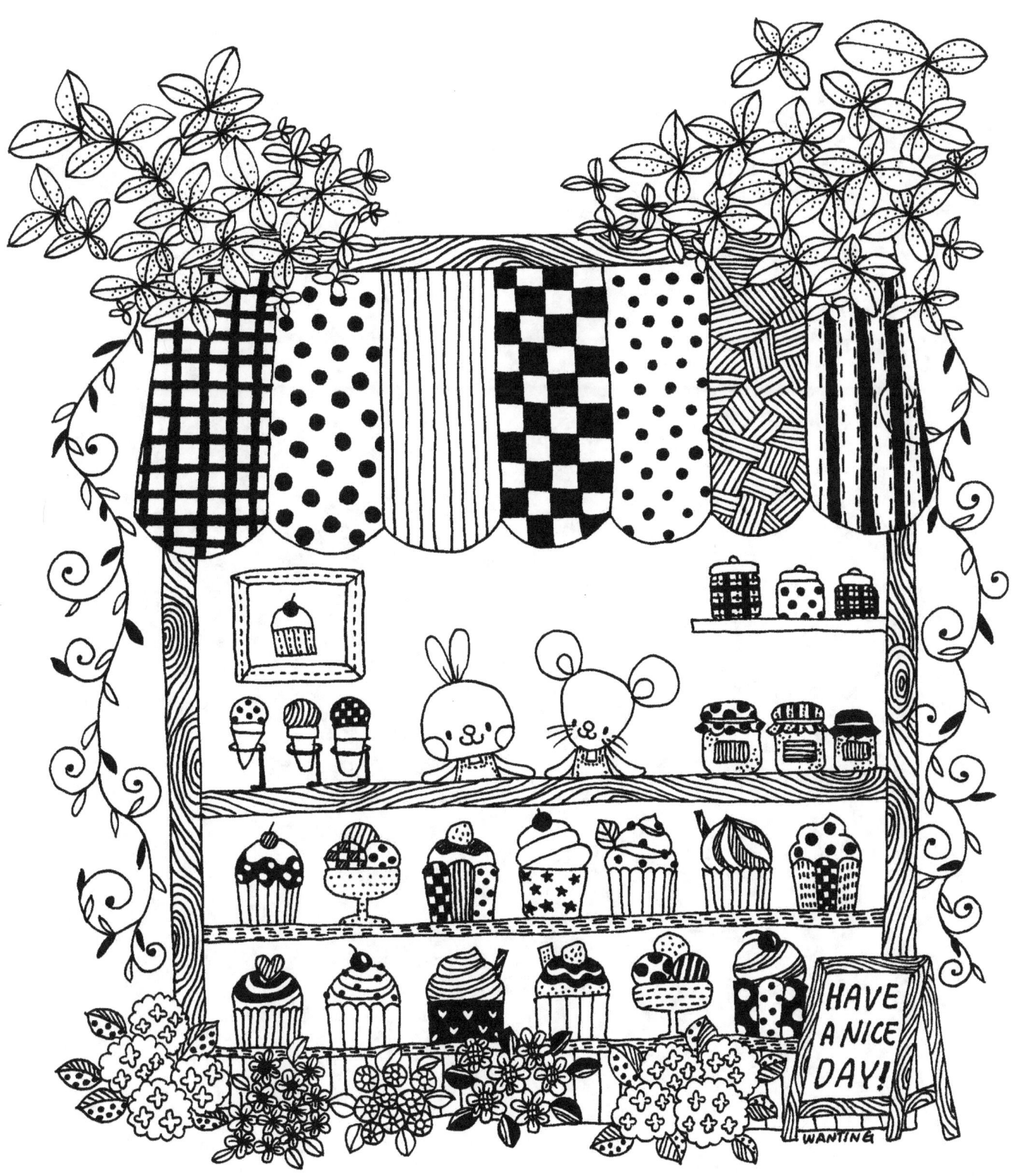

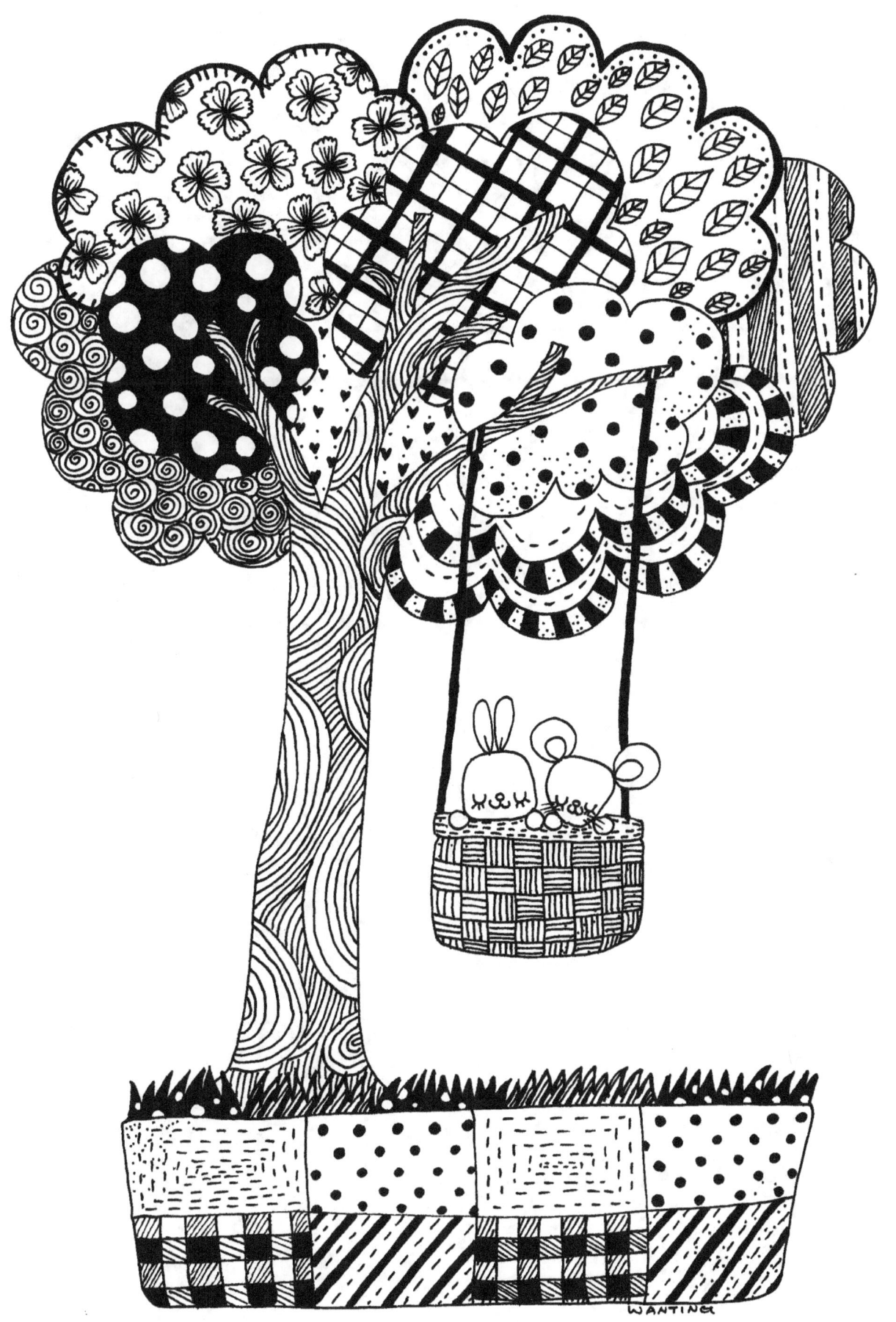

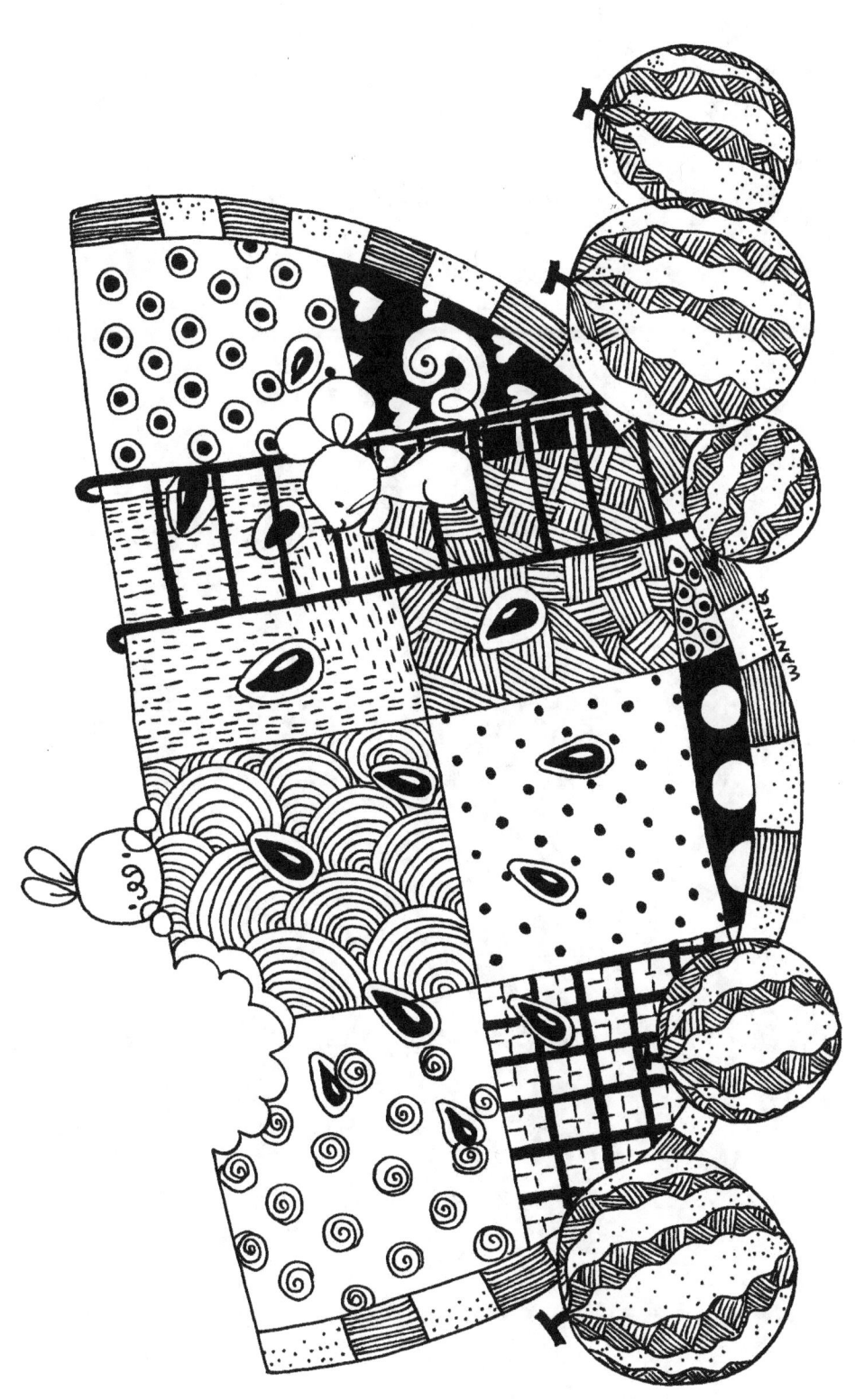

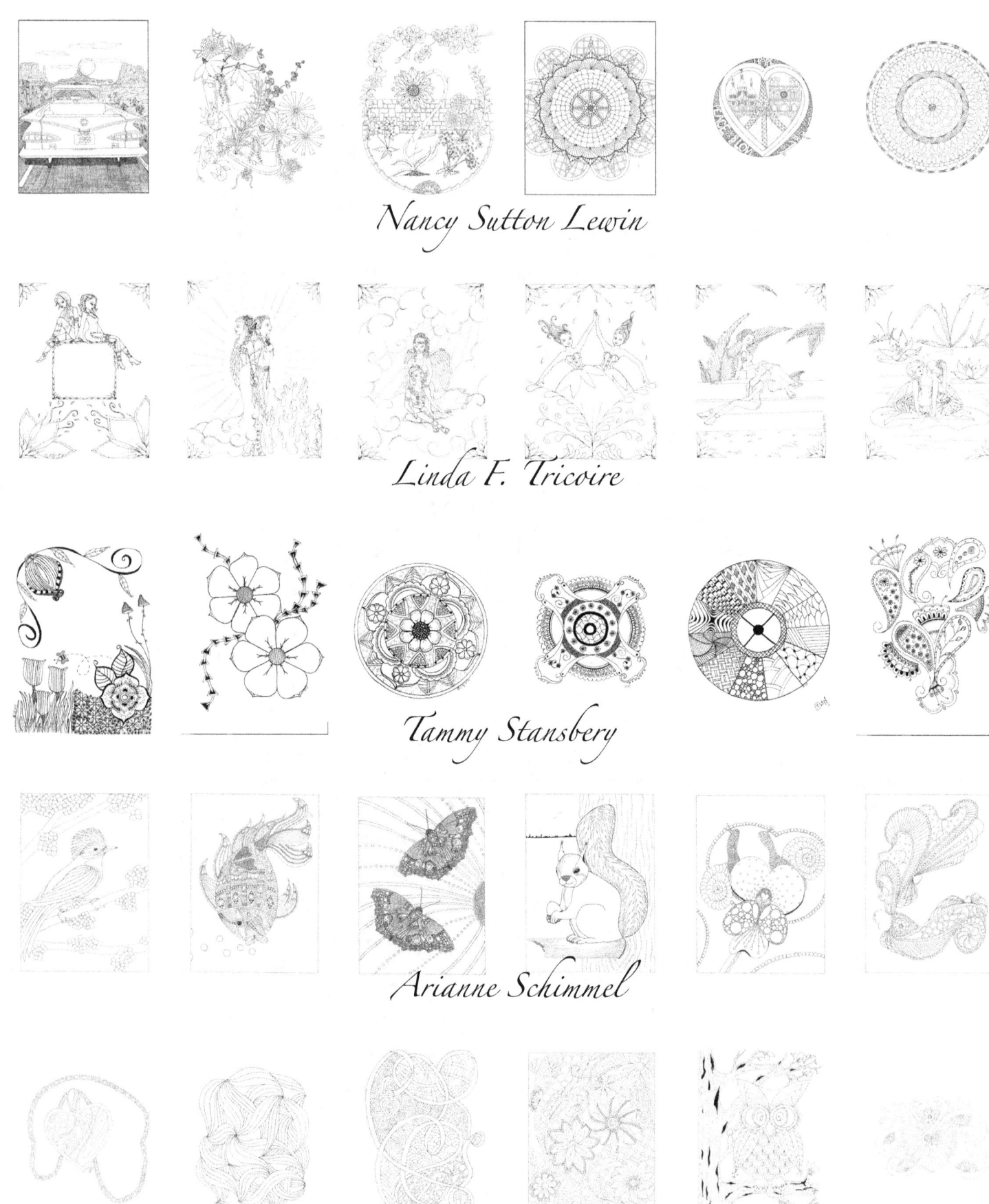

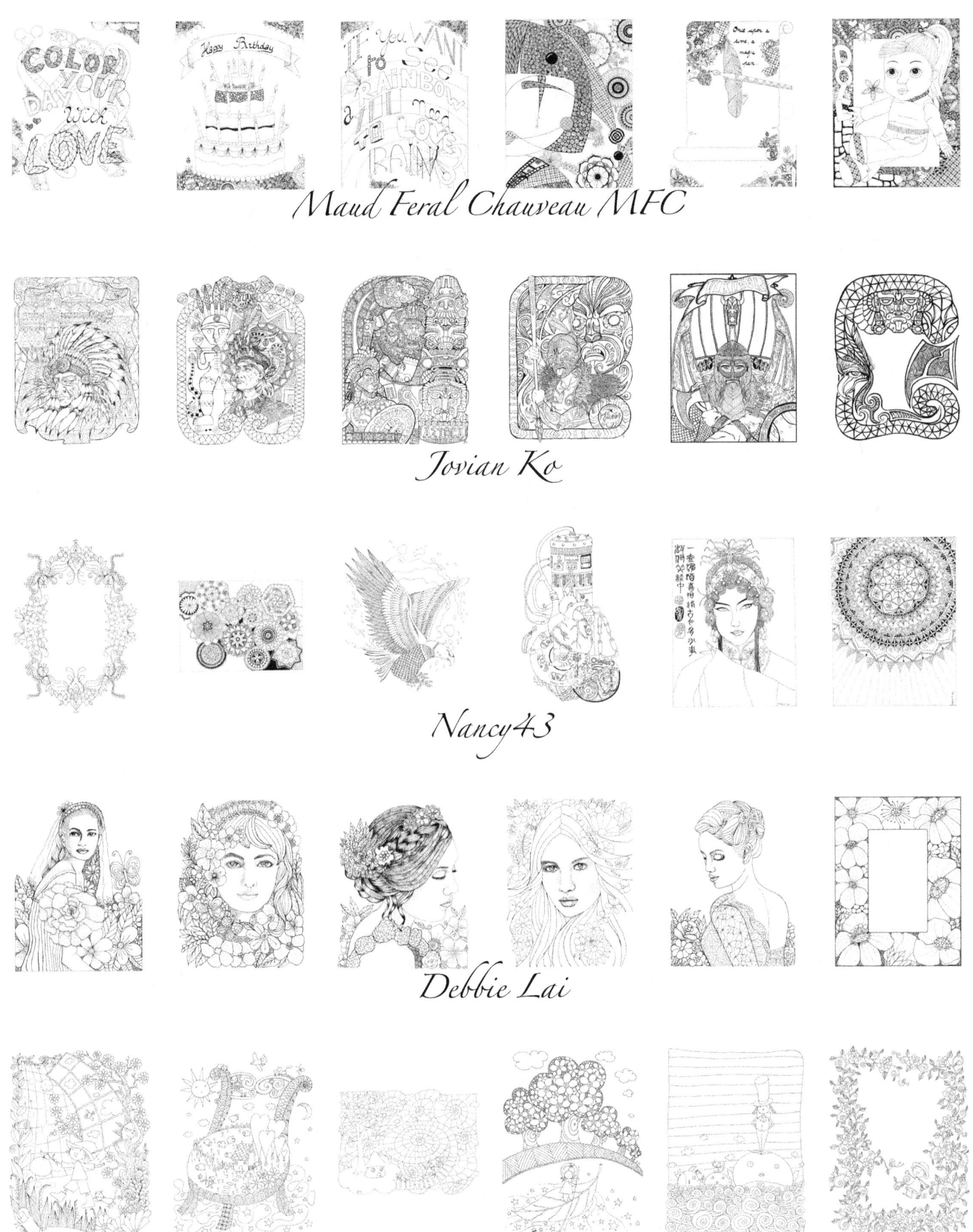

Maud Feral Chauveau MFC

Jovian Ko

Nancy43

Debbie Lai

Rover Hsiao

Test your colors here on the samples from
"My Pocket Coloring Companion"
&
"My Coloring Companion"

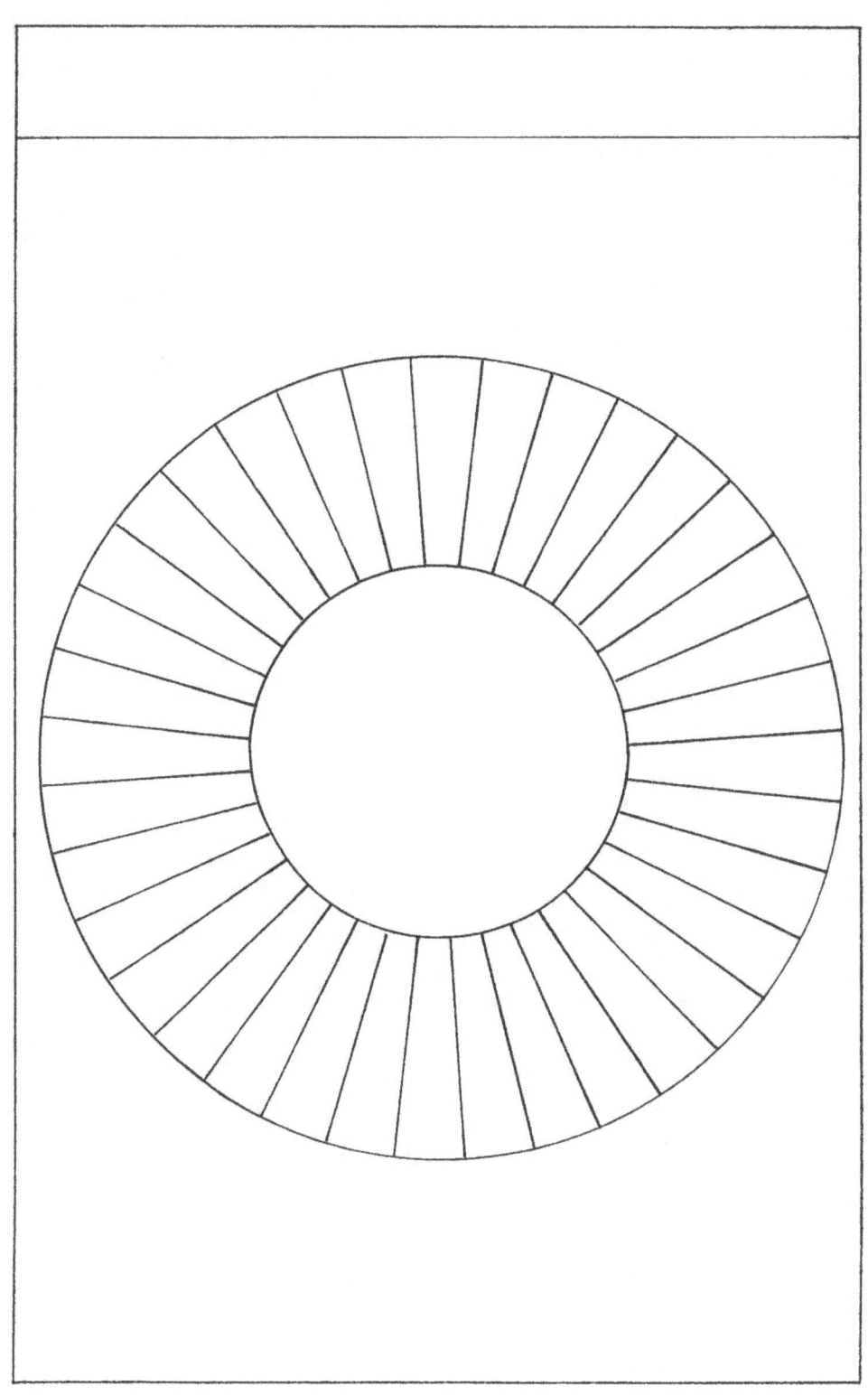

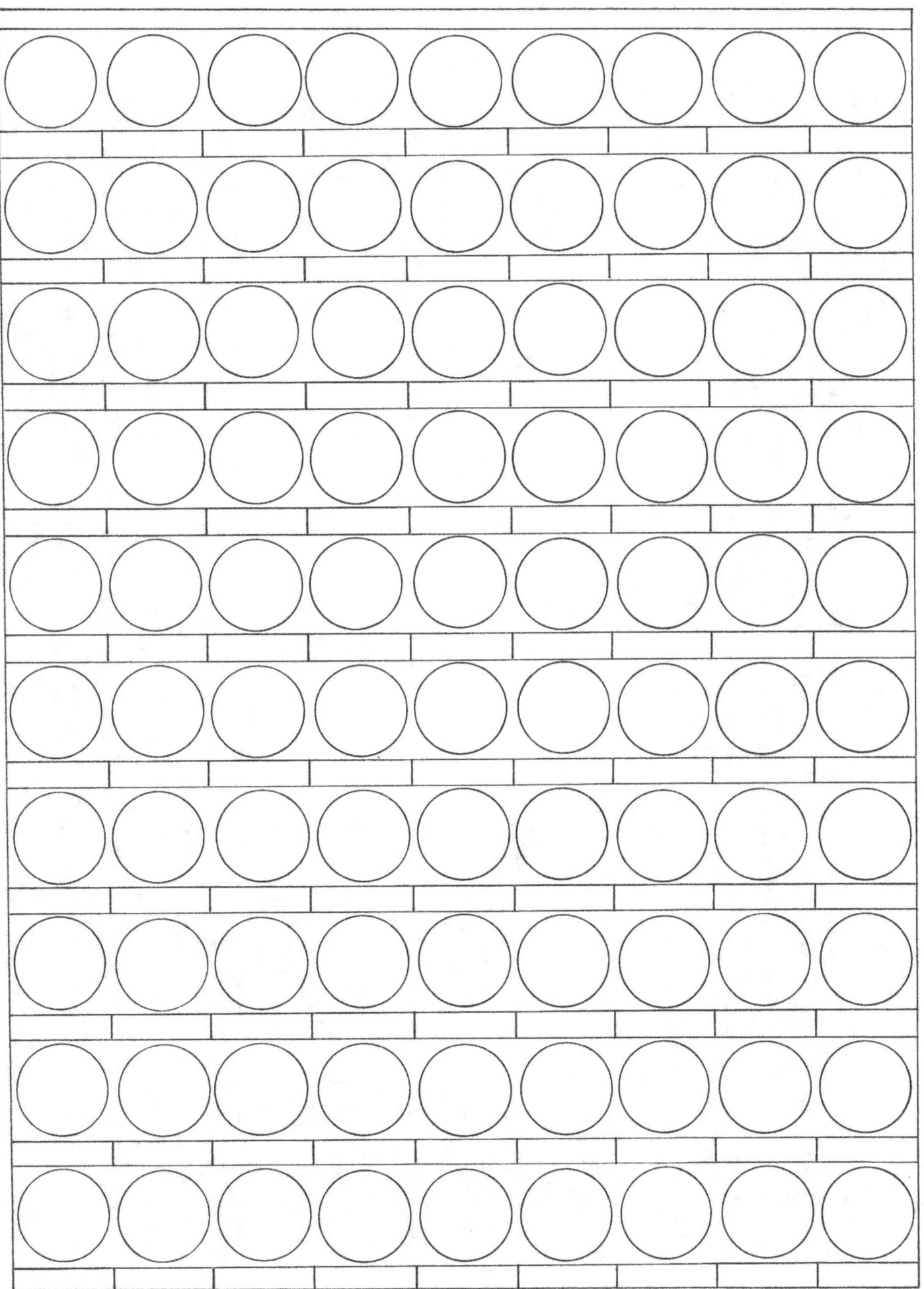

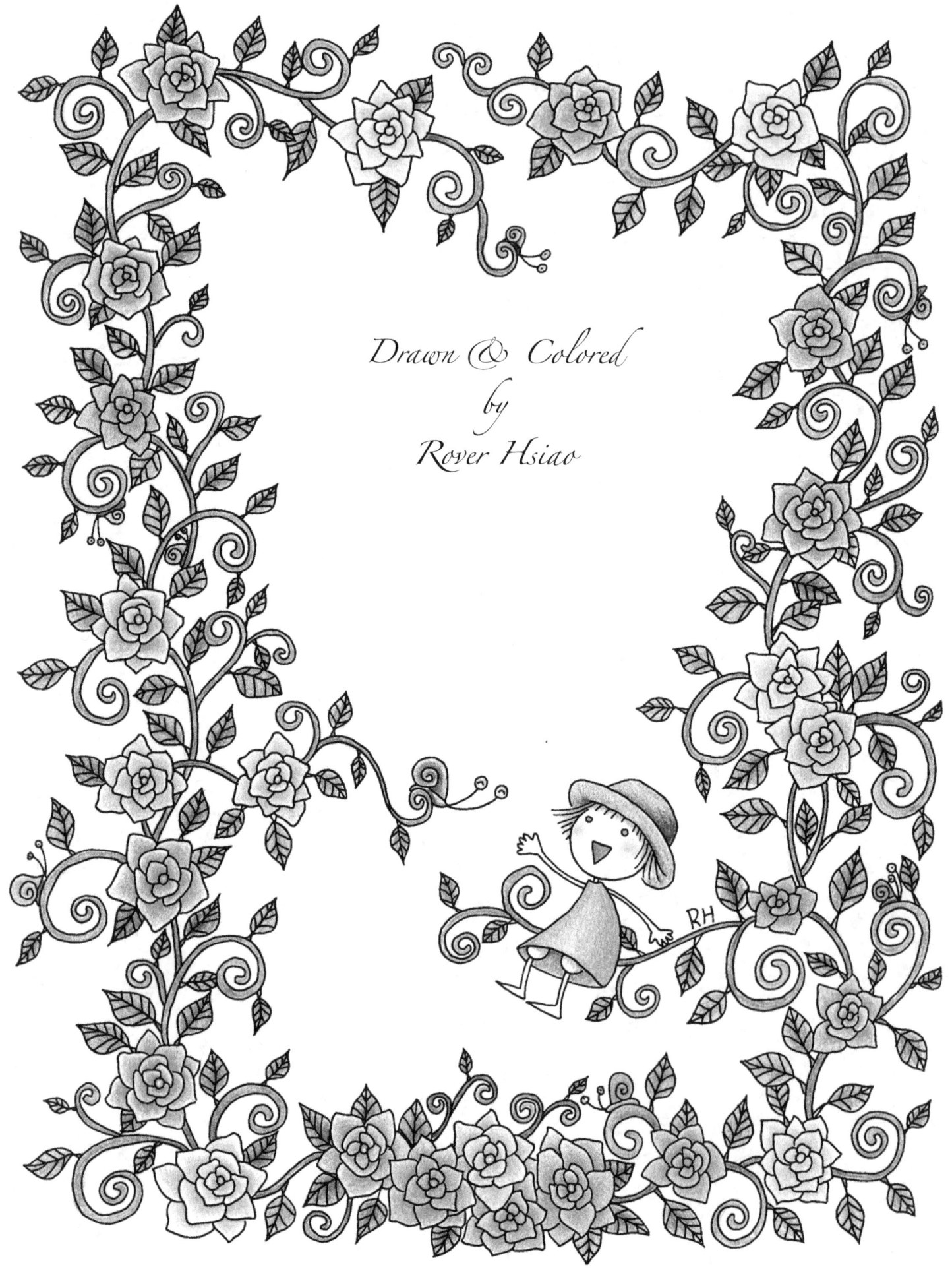